教育部基础学科拔尖学生培养计划 2.0 项目(20212060)
EFL Learning Series for Top-notch Innovative Talents
拔尖创新人才英语系列教材

思 辨 口 语

Critical Thinking in English

主　编　陈登峰　周小兰
副主编　左　宁　李　红　田庆强
编　者　王　静　张　帅　孙路平　程美丽

山东大学出版社
SHANDONG UNIVERSITY PRESS
·济南·

图书在版编目(CIP)数据

思辨口语:汉文、英文 / 陈登峰,周小兰主编. —
济南:山东大学出版社,2021.6(2023.9重印)
ISBN 978-7-5607-7060-4

Ⅰ. ①思… Ⅱ. ①陈… ②周… Ⅲ. ①英语—口语—
自学参考资料 Ⅳ. ①H319.9

中国版本图书馆 CIP 数据核字(2021)第 118174 号

责任编辑 李 璐
封面设计 牛 钧

出版发行 山东大学出版社
社　　址 山东省济南市山大南路 20 号
邮政编码 250100
发行热线 (0531)88363008
经　　销 新华书店
印　　刷 济南新科印务有限公司
规　　格 787 毫米×1092 毫米 1/16
　　　　 11.25 印张 249 千字
版　　次 2021 年 6 月第 1 版
印　　次 2023 年 9 月第 2 次印刷
定　　价 48.00 元

Contents

Unit 1 Education …… 1

Part A Parenting …… 1

A1. Introduction …… 1

A2. Passage Reading …… 3

Reference Words and Expressions …… 5

Speaking Activities …… 7

Reference Words and Expressions …… 10

Speaking Activities …… 12

A3. Extensive Reading …… 12

Part B School Education …… 15

B1. Introduction …… 15

B2. Passage Reading …… 20

Reference Words and Expressions …… 23

Speaking Activities …… 25

Reference Words and Expressions …… 29

Speaking Activities …… 30

B3. Extensive Reading …… 31

References …… 33

Unit 2 Psychology …… 35

Part A Happiness …… 35

A1. Introduction …… 35

A2. Passage Reading …… 37

Reference Words and Expressions …… 40

Speaking Activities …… 41

Reference Words and Expressions …… 45

Speaking Activities …… 46

A3. Extensive Reading ········· 47
Part B Stress ········· 49
B1. Introduction ········· 49
B2. Passage Reading ········· 52
Reference Words and Expressions ········· 54
Speaking Activities ········· 56
Reference Words and Expressions ········· 60
Speaking Activities ········· 62
B3. Extensive Reading ········· 63
References ········· 67

Unit 3 Technology ········· 69

Part A Technology and Human Health ········· 69
A1. Introduction ········· 69
A2. Passage Reading ········· 70
Reference Words and Expressions ········· 76
Speaking Activities ········· 77
Reference Words and Expressions ········· 83
Speaking Activities ········· 85
A3. Extensive Reading ········· 86
Part B Technology and Ethical Dilemmas ········· 88
B1. Introduction ········· 88
B2. Passage Reading ········· 88
Reference Words and Expressions ········· 94
Speaking Activities ········· 95
Reference Words and Expressions ········· 102
Speaking Activities ········· 103
B3. Extensive Reading ········· 104
References ········· 106

Unit 4 Environment ········· 108

Part A Pollution ········· 108
A1. Introduction ········· 108
A2. Passage Reading ········· 111
Reference Words and Expressions ········· 114
Speaking Activities ········· 116

Reference Words and Expressions ………… 120
Speaking Activities ………… 121
A3. Extensive Reading ………… 122
Part B Ecological Balance ………… 125
B1. Introduction ………… 125
B2. Passage Reading ………… 126
Reference Words and Expressions ………… 128
Speaking Activities ………… 130
Reference Words and Expressions ………… 133
Speaking Activities ………… 135
B3. Extensive Reading ………… 135
References ………… 137

Unit 5 Human ………… 140

Part A Personality and Quotient ………… 140
A1. Introduction ………… 140
A2. Passage Reading ………… 143
Reference Words and Expressions ………… 146
Speaking Activities ………… 147
Reference Words and Expressions ………… 151
Speaking Activities ………… 152
A3 Extensive Reading ………… 153
Part B Gender and Age ………… 157
B1. Introduction ………… 157
B2. Passage Reading ………… 158
Reference Words and Expressions ………… 161
Speaking Activities ………… 162
Reference Words and Expressions ………… 166
Speaking Activities ………… 168
B3. Extensive Reading ………… 168
References ………… 171

Unit 1 Education

Part A Parenting

A1. Introduction

Types of Parenting

Authoritarian parenting

Authoritarian parents believe kids should follow the rules without exception.

Authoritarian parents are famous for saying "because I said so" when a child questions the reasons behind a rule. They are not interested in negotiating and their focus is on obedience. They also don't allow kids to get involved in problem-solving challenges or obstacles. Instead, they make the rules and enforce the consequences with little regard for a child's opinion.

Authoritarian parents may use punishments instead of discipline. So rather than teach kids how to make better choices, they're invested in making kids feel sorry for their mistakes.

Children who grow up with strict authoritarian parents tend to follow rules much of the time. But their obedience comes at a price. Children of authoritarian parents are at a higher risk of developing self-esteem problems because their opinions aren't valued.

They may also become hostile or aggressive. Rather than think about how to do things better in the future, they often focus on the anger they feel toward their parents. Since authoritarian parents are often strict, their children may grow to become good liars in an effort to avoid punishment.

Authoritative parenting

Authoritative parents have rules and they use consequences, but they also take their children's opinions into account. They validate their children's feelings, while also making it clear that the adults are ultimately in charge.

Authoritative parents invest time and energy into preventing behavior problems before they start. They also use positive discipline strategies to reinforce good behavior, like praise and reward systems.

Researchers have found kids who have authoritative parents are most likely to become responsible adults who feel comfortable expressing their opinions. Children raised with authoritative discipline tend to be happy and successful. They're also more likely to be good at making decisions and evaluating safety risks on their own.

Permissive parenting

Permissive parents are lenient. They often only step in when there's a serious problem.

They're quite forgiving and they adopt an attitude of "kids will be kids". When they do use consequences, they may not make those consequences stick. They might give privileges back if a child begs or they may allow a child to get out of time-out early if he promises to be good.

Permissive parents usually take on more of a friend role than a parent role. They often encourage their children to talk with them about their problems, but they usually don't put much effort into discouraging poor choices or bad behavior.

Kids who grow up with permissive parents are more likely to struggle academically. They may exhibit more behavioral problems as they don't appreciate authority and rules. They often have low self-esteem and may report a lot of sadness.

They're also at a higher risk for health problems, like obesity, because permissive parents struggle to limit junk food intake. They are even more likely to have dental cavities because permissive parents often don't enforce good habits, like ensuring a child brushes his teeth.

Uninvolved parenting

Uninvolved parents tend to have little knowledge of what their children are doing. There tend to be few rules. Children may not receive much guidance, nurturing, and parental attention.

Uninvolved parents expect children to raise themselves. They don't devote much time or energy to meeting children's basic needs.

Uninvolved parents may be neglectful but it's not always intentional. A parent with mental health issues or substance abuse problems, for example, may not be able to care for children's physical or emotional needs on a consistent basis.

At other times, uninvolved parents lack knowledge about child development. And sometimes, they're simply overwhelmed with other problems, like work, paying bills, and managing a household.

Children with uninvolved parents are likely to struggle with self-esteem issues. They tend to perform poorly in school. They also exhibit frequent behavior problems and rank low in happiness.

(Adapted from *verywellfamily.com*)

A2. Passage Reading

A2.1 Different Parenting Styles

The following two passages focus on different extremes of parenting styles. Read and give your opinions according to the questions. Try to seek diverse perspectives and don't confine yourself to the reference words and expressions given.

Passage One

"Tiger Mothers" Leave Lifelong Scars

Lac Su

All my young life, my parents were **quick to remind** me of my stupidity. Their burning desire to see me achieve at any cost resulted in the same **belittling** imparted by Chua (author of *Battle Hymn of the Tiger Mother*) on her daughters. My parents were particularly **preoccupied with** my lack of progress in school.

Fixated on the idea that I was **a slow learner**, they confused my cautiousness with a lack of desire, and my need for affection as the wants of a spoiled American brat. In telling me that I was a stupid, worthless, waste of space, they believed they were **spurning** me on to do great things. Like Chua's daughters, they didn't allow time with friends, and no matter how hard I worked, or how **dutifully** I **obeyed** their commands. It was never enough.

Three years ago, during a family gathering, my father **confessed regret** about his choice in parenting. I didn't know what to say. The **damage** had been done.

I feel for Chua's daughters and imagine they'll have similar conversations with her one day. Chua doesn't seem to wonder if her **tiger techniques** are **overboard**, and neither did my father while I was young. He never asked if the **abuse** was unwarranted, and never questioned whether isolating me from the world was the best way for me to learn how to **maneuver in** it. In his mind, he had done the right thing.

Only by seeing me as an adult, **taking a nurturing, accepting approach** in rearing my children, did my father realize that there is a better way.

Now in my mid-thirties, I'm sure I appear successful and happy **on the surface.** I'm a published author, a successful executive, and I have a Ph. D. in psychology. In spite of this, my parents' approach failed. I'm torn to pieces **on the inside.** I've been through countless hours of psychotherapy, and my **lack of self-worth** beckons me to rely on alcohol to numb the pain.

I should be chasing my dreams, not chasing pain.

Children need their parents' love and acceptance in order to **develop real self-esteem.** Belittling children sends the message that they are not worthy of love and support—as do **mind games, emotional abuse, and tight-fisted control.**

This message lasts a lifetime. I still question every day if I am, indeed, stupid. I didn't even raise my hand in class until graduate school because I honestly believed that a moron like me has nothing worthy to say.

If I could say one thing to Amy Chua, it's that I would trade every last bit of my success in life to live without the deep wounds given to me by a Tiger Mother.

(Adapted from *cnn. com*)

☞**Note**

Battle Hymn of the Tiger Mother: A book written by American author and Yale law professor Amy Chua that was published in 2011. It quickly popularized the concept and term "tiger mother" while also becoming the inspiration for TV shows and dramas in many countries. In the book, Chua recounts her efforts to give her children what she describes as a traditional, strict "Chinese" upbringing. This piece was controversial. Many readers believed that Chua was advocating the "superiority" of a particular, very strict, ethnically-defined approach to parenting.

Passage Two

How Parents Are Robbing Their Children of Adulthood

Claire C. Miller and Jonah E. Bromwich

Helicopter parenting, the practice of **hovering anxiously** near one's children, **monitoring** their every activity, is so 20th century. Some affluent mothers and fathers now are more like snowplows: machines chugging ahead, **clearing any obstacles** in their child's path to success, so they don't have to **encounter failure, frustration or lose opportunities.**

Taken to its criminal extreme, it means bribing SAT proctors and paying off college coaches to get children into **elite colleges** and then **going to great lengths** to make sure they never face the humiliation of knowing how they got there.

It starts early, when parents get on wait lists for **elite preschools** before their babies are born and try to make sure their toddlers never do anything that may frustrate them. It gets more intense when school starts: running a forgotten assignment to school or calling a coach to request that their child make the team.

Later, it's writing them an excuse if they **procrastinate on** schoolwork, paying a college counselor thousands of dollars to **perfect their applications** or calling their professors to **argue about a grade.** In colleges, many students rely on their parents to set up play dates with people in their dorm or complain to their employers when an internship didn't lead to a job. The root cause was parents who had never let their children make mistakes or **face challenges.**

Yes, it's a parent's job to support the children, and to use their **adult wisdom** to prepare for the future when their children aren't mature enough to do so. That's why parents hide certain toys from toddlers to avoid temper tantrums or take away a teenager's car keys until he finishes his college applications. But snowplow parents can **take it too far**, some experts say.

If children have never **faced an obstacle**, what happens when they get into the real world? Learning to **solve problems**, **take risks** and **overcome frustration** are crucial life skills, many child development experts say, and if parents don't let their children **encounter failure**, the children don't acquire them.

Snowplowing has gone so far that many young people are in crisis, lacking these problem-solving skills and experiencing record rates of anxiety.

(Adapted from *nytimes. com*)

Opinion sharing

(a) Summarize the traits of the two ways of child-rearing respectively.
(b) What is your parents' parenting style like?
(c) If you have to choose between a tiger parent and a snowplow parent, which type of parents would you prefer? Give reasons.
(d) Do you know any other parenting styles? Describe them.
(e) Talk about your ideal way of upbringing.

Reference Words and Expressions

conflict	冲突，矛盾
democratic	民主的
threaten	威胁，恐吓

rank	排名，等级
unconditional	无条件的，绝对的
requirement	要求
push	催促
self-confidence	自信
self-esteem	自尊
privacy	隐私
forge	锻造，铸造
hands-off	不干涉，不插手
indulgence	放纵
sleepover	在朋友家过夜，夜不归宿
enforce	实施，执行，强制
rebellious	反抗的，造反的
provocative	挑拨的，煽动性的
independence	独立
obedient	顺从的，服从的
abusive	辱骂的，滥用的，虐待的

tiger mom	“虎妈”
a strict disciplinarian parent	严厉管教的父母
dominating traits	主要特征
authoritarian parenting	专制型父母
parenting philosophy	育儿哲学
demand high achievements	要求高的成就
shape their behavior	塑造他们的行为
high expectations	高期望
academic pursuits	学术追求
live up to one’s potential	发挥自己的潜力
solidly move one’s way up	稳步向上
assume strength rather than fragility	要坚强不要脆弱
stimulate the development of creativity	激发创造力的发展
stifle one’s creativity	扼杀一个人的创造力
inhibit critical thinking	抑制批判性思维
gain supremacy in study	在学习上占上风
studious kids	好学的孩子
academic achievement	学术成就
physical violence	身体暴力
post grades	公开成绩

lack authority	缺乏权威
micro manage	细微化管理
mom's boy	"妈宝"
fevered debate	激烈的争论
tough love strategy	严厉的爱策略
extracurricular activities	课外活动
reward and punishment	赏罚,奖惩
refrain from criticizing	避免批评
take the side of	支持
stir up self-doubt	激发自我怀疑

Speaking Activities

Monologue

Upon your 18th birthday, your parents are preparing a big celebration, while you are lost in thought. At this very moment, before stepping into adulthood, you really would like to say something to your parents. Express your feelings towards their parenting.

Read and discuss

College Admissions Scandal

In 2019, a scandal arose over a criminal conspiracy to influence undergraduate admissions decisions at several top American universities. At least 53 people have been charged as part of the conspiracy, a number of whom pleaded guilty or agreed to plead guilty. Thirty-three parents of college applicants are accused of paying more than 25 million dollars between 2011 and 2018 to someone who used part of the money to fraudulently inflate entrance exam test scores and bribe college officials.

(Adapted from *marca.com*)

(a) According to the news, 31 accused parents tried to cheat their way to get their children admitted to elite universities. What type of parents do you think they are in child rearing? Talk about how they might have raised their children.

(b) Why can't the parents let their children work their way to the universities on their own merits? Do you think their children agree with their behavior?

Read and discuss

Sheng Enyi was the favorite son of Sheng Xuanhuai, once the richest man in the Republic of China. Enyi was born in 1892 and was sent to prestigious overseas schools at a young age. He then returned to China, where his father made him director of his companies.

With such abundant inheritance, Sheng Enyi didn't work hard to develop his family business, but was addicted to gambling. In the end, he lost every penny gambling and was starved to death.

(a) What do you think of Sheng Xuanhuai's parenting style?
(b) Why did Sheng Enyi lose everything even though he was highly educated?
(c) To avoid this kind of tragedy, what should rich parents do?

A2.2 The Role of Father and Mother

The following two passages focus on the role of father and mother in family education. Read and give your opinions according to the questions. Try to seek diverse perspectives and don't confine yourself to the reference words and expressions given.

Passage One

Father Absence

According to the 2007 UNICEF report on the well-being of children in economically advanced nations, children in the U. S., Canada and the U. K. rank extremely low in regard to social and emotional well-being in particular. Many theories have been explored to explain the poor state of our nation's children. However, a factor that has been largely ignored, particularly among child and family policymakers, is the **prevalence and devastating effects** of father absence in children's lives.

For starters, studies repeatedly show that children without fathers **positively present** in the home suffer greatly. Even before a child is born, their father's attitudes regarding the pregnancy, behaviors during the prenatal period, and the relationship between their father and mother may **indirectly influence** the risk for **adverse** birth outcomes. In early childhood, studies show that school-aged children with good relationships with their fathers were less likely to **experience depression**, to **exhibit disruptive behavior**, or to lie. Overall, they were far more likely to exhibit **prosocial behavior.**

In adolescence, the implications of fatherless homes are incredible. Former President George W. Bush even addressed the issue while in office, stating, "Over the past four decades, fatherlessness has emerged as one of our greatest social problems. We know that children who grow up with absent-fathers can **suffer lasting damage**. They are more likely to **end up in poverty** or **drop out of school**, become **addicted to drugs**, **have a child out of wedlock**, or **end up in prison**. Fatherlessness is not the only cause of these things, but our nation must recognize it is an important factor."

Narratively speaking, many individuals can attest to the fact that the lasting impact of a father in child's life cannot be denied. Many would admit that they have struggled with **feelings of abandonment** and **low self-esteem**, due to the lack of a father's love in their lives. Some have turned to drugs, alcohol, risky sexual activities, unhealthy relationships, or other **destructive behaviors** to numb the pains of fatherlessness.

Although the absence of their father is not an isolated risk factor, it definitely can **take a toll on** the development of children.

(Adapted from *all 4 kids. org*)

Passage Two

A Mother's Influence

Sara Horn

Caleb, my 12-year-old son, stormed into the kitchen and sat at the counter with a scowl as he declared, "I'm so tired of Tim — he always gets everything he asks for. It's not fair!"

I'd never seen Caleb so upset. Tim was a family friend, and it was true that his family liked to buy things. Although I understood why our family saves for things, in my heart I had to agree that it was hard being around others who didn't have to wait for what they wanted.

Still, as much as I wanted to agree about the unfairness of it all, I knew there could be a lesson for my son — a lesson about the satisfaction that comes with earning something. I knew that my mothering in this moment had the **potential to be influential**, so I reminded Caleb about the math test he'd just aced.

"You worked pretty hard for that grade, didn't you?" I asked him. He stared back as he nodded, a stern expression still on his face. I returned a sympathetic smile and continued, "If your teacher just gave that A to you, would it mean as much?"

I watched Caleb's scowl soften as he looked down, thinking about my words. Caleb agreed with me that we shouldn't want what others have, but he still struggled to appreciate the value of contentment. Some lessons take longer to learn than others.

Influencing Caleb to think wisely is **a daily challenge**. As a mom, I don't ever **have the luxury to be "off"**. Every day I **set the example** with my words, whether they're **loving or harsh**; by my actions, whether they're kind or selfish; even by my decisions, whether they're right or wrong.

Just think about the **impact** our choices have on our children. What do they notice when we talk on the phone with a friend? Are we an encouragement or a gossip? When we watch television — does it take time away from family time? Or when we interact with people in public — are we polite or rude?

Influence starts with availability. **Intentional availability** — fully present. We can be in the same room as our children and not really paying attention to them. Consider sitting next to your kids when they're watching a movie, or inviting them to help cook dinner. A mother's presence in her children's lives means more to them than we know and **sets the foundation for** relationship in years to come.

It's often easier to **spot the flaws** in our kids than to **be sensitive to** what they're doing well. Make a point to encourage your child in what she does right and not just correct her when she does wrong. It's best for us to **be direct in our actions** but **cautious in our reactions**, helping our kids believe that we will be their **lifelong cheerleader.**

(Adapted from *focusonthefamily.com*)

Opinion sharing

(a) Summarize the influence of father and mother in children's growth respectively. What impact will it have on the child if the father or mother is absent?
(b) How have your father influenced you? And your mother?
(c) Does the parents' state of wealth affect the way of education of their kids? Why? Give examples to illustrate.
(d) What kind of father or mother do you want to be in the future?
(e) Do you have any suggestion for single-parent family in minimizing negative influence on their children?

Reference Words and Expressions

detrimental	有害的,不利的
repercussion	反响,弹回
self-control	自控
sacrifice	牺牲
depression	沮丧,抑郁症
father / mother involvement / engagement	父亲/母亲参与教养
gender roles	性别角色
produce confusion	产生混乱
gendered behavior	性别行为
have consistent effects on	对……有一致的影响
have an extraordinary influence	具有非凡的影响力
childhood role models	童年的榜样
send a clear and powerful message	发出清晰有力的信息

development of children	孩子的发展
cognitive skills and behaviors	认知技能和行为
physical and emotional security	身体和情绪安全
lower the educational attainment	降低受教育程度
decrease the likelihood	降低可能性
place someone at a major disadvantage	使某人处于非常不利的地位
mental health	心理健康
personal happiness	个人幸福
have lasting effects on	对……有持久的影响
be emotionally attached to	情感上依附于
be actively involved with	积极参与
balance work and family life	平衡工作和家庭生活
feel a closeness to	对……感到亲近
in times of adversity	在逆境中
a critical role	一个关键的角色
hinder development	阻碍发展
psychological harm	心理伤害
academic achievement	学术成就
behavioral adjustment	行为调整
quality of relationship	关系质量
high / low levels of confidence	自信程度高/低
act out	把……表演出来，把……付诸行动
risky behaviors	危险行为
frequency of problems	问题频率
reduce psychological problems	减少心理问题
juvenile delinquency	青少年犯罪
take a toll on	给……造成重大伤害（或损失）
drug and alcohol abuse	药物与酒精滥用
truancy and academic performance	旷课和学业表现
physical health problems	身体健康问题
future relationships	未来关系
strengthen the bond	加强纽带
handle embarrassment	处理尴尬
initiate meaningful dialogues	发起有意义的对话
long-lasting benefits	长期利益
emotional, academic, social and behavioral outcomes	情感、学术、社会和行为结果

Speaking Activities

Brainstorm

In traditional Chinese family, many parents try to maintain their marriages even when they no longer have affection for each other. The main reason is the fear of negative influence on their children's psychological health.

(a) Brainstorm the possible negative influence of a divorce.

(b) Share your opinions on whether a divorce is necessary for a couple with kids when their relationship turns sour.

Discussion

(a) There is a famous story in ancient China "Three Moves by Mencius' Mother", which is about a wise mother who tried to find a good environment for her child's best education. Discuss the significance of the action of Mencius' mother. Do you approve of her way of raising a child? Why?

(b) In China, many families suffer from the "busy father, frustrated mother syndrome". Can you analyze the root causes for this phenomenon in depth? How to reverse the situation and restore balance to father and mother involvement in a family? Give suggestions.

Debate

In China, more and more moms are working. Working moms might not be as involved in child rearing as those stay-at-home moms. Who do you think can do a better job at parenting?

Topic for debate: stay-at-home moms do a better job at parenting.

A3. Extensive Reading

Five Tips for Successful Parenting

Being a parent is one of the most challenging tasks of your life and successful parenting involves a fundamental desire to learn and improve your parenting skills. This is especially true when it comes to child discipline. While children are adorable to play with, teaching them right from wrong, and good from bad, can be tough.

As parents, we usually end up in a power struggle because we are worried the children will get hurt, or break something, or make a mess, etc. Successful parenting involves knowing when to get into a power struggle, and when to walk away from one because it just isn't worth the fight.

"Power struggle" may sound harsh, but this is what exactly happens when you try to dress your children and they just scream "No! No!" What's bad about this is that nobody wins, and both parties can end up hating each other.

Believe it or not, there is a way to raise a child without being too stressed about it. Your kid can be your friend if you follow these tips for successful parenting.

Give your child space

No individual wants to be controlled. It's true for children also. This is one of the first things a parent needs to understand in raising responsible, happy children. Every person wants to have a "say" over himself, and that's something we all need to respect. Giving your children the freedom to decide on what shirt or shoes he wants to wear is a very good step in showing that you respect his decision.

Now, there is a fine line between giving space and giving him the freedom to do anything that he pleases. As a parent, you are responsible for raising your child and helping guide him to make good choices. But you need to do it in such a way that you don't violate his self-being. If you don't like his choice of leaving his toys around, explain the natural consequences of it and stick to it.

Compliment your children

Compliments can boost self-confidence, and this is probably something you'd like for your child, right? How much confidence a person has often determines if they will be successful in life, especially when it comes to managing a career.

When you give compliments, always make sure that it is genuine. Compliments need to be earned, and this is something that your child needs to understand. Otherwise, they may incorrectly learn that they'll get a compliment form you without earning it. And this belief could extend to other people your child interacts with down the road.

The important thing to remember here is to compliment your child whenever you see that he has exerted effort on what he's doing, and not just praise him for something simple. If your child succeeds at something simple like putting away some toys, say "thanks" instead of complimenting it. Make it at least slightly challenging to earn the compliment!

Spend quality time with your children

Life is busy, no doubt. But no matter what, you need to make time for your children. Too many parents fail to do this and not only do they feel guilty later, but the children take notice and it affects their behavior.

Make no mistake that no matter how busy you feel your life is, you are CHOOSING to either spend your time with your children or somewhere else. Choose the right balance.

Avoid the regret that you'll surely feel otherwise.

Spending time with your children also allows you to understand their motivations and likes or dislikes. This will help you when it comes to discipline later.

Positive communication

Some parents only tend to have "serious conversations" with their kids when they misbehave. The focus of the conversation is around what parents want their kids NOT to do.

Let's not forget that kids also grow and benefit from hearing what you appreciate about them. And speaking in positive terms really helps here. Even if you are trying to correct poor behavior, it's more effective to tell your child what you DO want rather than what you don't want.

Also, remember to talk with your kids, rather than at them. Listen to your kids' opinion and feelings. Ask good questions when something is unclear. You'll be surprised how smart your kids actually are, and you'll learn something you didn't already know.

Talking with your kids also fosters a feeling of love.

Learn from your mistakes

We all want to be the perfect parent, but there's just no such thing. In order to be a successful parent, we need to learn from our own mistakes. Mistakes are how we learn, and if we don't make mistakes we are not learning. But if we make mistakes without acknowledging them, we also fail to learn.

If you are trying to develop a certain behavior in a child and are not having success, try something else. Don't keep trying to get your result with the same (failing) method. Adapt. Think about how your child is motivated and try something new. Otherwise, you'll not only fail to accomplish the change that you are after, but you'll strain your relationship with your kids.

Above all, successful parenting is achieved when a loving and caring parent is able to observe what is working, and modify what is not working.

(Adapted from *parentingcode.com*)

Part B School Education

B1. Introduction

Why Is Education Crucial?

Education means studying in order to obtain a deeper knowledge and understanding of a variety of subjects to be applied to daily life. Education is not limited to just knowledge from books, but can also be obtained through practical experiences outside of the classroom.

Children are the future of our world, making education crucial for them. Their knowledge is what's going to keep our world alive and flourishing.

At childhood

During the childhood development stages, the importance of education is stronger than ever. It's a time for children to learn social and mental skills that will be crucial for their growth and success in the future. Education at childhood also offers a chance for self-discovery and to learn about their unique interests.

The role

The importance of education in our lives goes far beyond what we can read in a textbook. Education also provides with knowledge such as how to produce artwork and make music. Education allows us to analyze what's in front of us, and even learn from our mistakes.

Goal building

By learning from a young age, children are given the chance to start building goals for themselves. Education means having the logic to set your mind to something and achieve it.

(Adapted from *uopeople.edu*)

Why Is a College Education So Important?

A college education is important for many students because it opens the doors to opportunities they would not have otherwise; it helps young people grow into adulthood and it raises the college graduates' income throughout the rest of their lives. In addition, college teaches students to learn to think creatively and analytically, as well as learn skills that are useful in the job market and in life.

A study by the Organization for Economic Cooperation and Development shows that the economic return on a college education is an average of 12.3 percent for men, far higher than a typical return for stock market investments. College graduates earn, on average, 50 percent more than non-graduates.

College provides a venue for making connections and building networks that graduates could not build any other way, increasing their access and opportunities once they enter the job market. Many employers require or desire a college degree in their new hires, particularly during tough economic times. This effectively closes the door to certain jobs for those who have not graduated from college.

People who lack college degrees are more likely to be limited to basic jobs in service, manufacturing and construction industries. While employees with a high school education may secure jobs with good benefits, college graduates enter higher-level careers with greater salaries. They are also more likely to receive promotions, earn raises and develop reasoning and communication skills that can be applied to their jobs.

In addition, college exposes students to learning, projects and extracurricular activities they would probably never get in another environment. Students also make friends through their common bonding experiences, some of whom are likely to stay friends for the rest of their lives. College is also important because students learn to deal with competition, develop lifelong interests and develop confidence through their college achievements.

During their classes, college students often develop the reasoning skills needed to make life decisions, ranging from buying a home to helping their children choose their own college. In fact, college graduates are more likely to have children who also complete a college education. Other advantages of educational degrees may include better study habits and so-called "soft skills" which spell out into communication and collaborative and cooperative behaviors that enable humans to not only de-escalate dangerous and potential fatal situations, but also negotiate for advantageous placement of self and those close to oneself even in the face of overwhelming obstacles or unfair disadvantages. When others react with anger or despair, those who have a broad palate of interpersonal skills and coping mechanisms will be successful by persevering, analyzing and assessing the status quo and strategizing towards a new outcome. These are all skills taught in college in various courses such as Algebra, History, Sociology and Philosophy for instance, also known as General Education, or the Humanities.

(Adapted from *reference.com*; *study.com*)

Different Teaching Styles

The authority / lecture style

The authority model is teacher-centered and frequently entails lengthy lecture sessions or one-way presentations. Students are expected to take notes or absorb information.

Pros: This style is acceptable for certain higher-education disciplines and auditorium settings with large groups of students. The pure lecture style is most suitable for subjects like history, which necessitate memorization of key facts, dates, names, etc.

Cons: It's a questionable model for teaching children because there is little or no interaction with the teacher. Plus it can get a little snoozy. That's why it's a better approach for older, more mature students.

The demonstrator / coach style

The demonstrator retains the formal authority role by showing students what they need to know. The demonstrator is a lot like the lecturer, but their lessons include multimedia presentations, activities, and demonstrations.

Pros: This style gives teachers opportunities to incorporate a variety of formats including lectures and multimedia presentations.

Cons: Although it's well-suited for teaching mathematics, music, physical education, or arts and crafts, it is difficult to accommodate students' individual needs in larger classrooms.

The facilitator / activity style

Facilitators promote self-learning and help students develop critical thinking skills and retain knowledge that leads to self-actualization.

Pros: This style trains students to ask questions and helps develop skills to find answers and solutions through exploration; it is ideal for teaching science and similar subjects.

Cons: It challenges the teacher to interact with students and prompt them toward discovery rather than lecturing facts and testing knowledge through memorization. So, it's a bit harder to measure success in tangible terms.

The delegator / group style

The delegator style is best suited for curricula that require lab activities, such as chemistry and biology, or subjects that warrant peer feedback, like debate and creative writing.

Pros: Guided discovery and inquiry-based learning place the teacher in an observer role that inspires students by working in tandem toward common goals.

Cons: Considered a modern style of teaching, it is sometimes criticized as eroding teacher authority. As a delegator, the teacher acts more as a consultant rather than the traditional authority figure.

The hybrid / blended style

Hybrid, or blended style, follows an integrated approach to teaching that blends the teacher's personality and interests with students' needs and curriculum-appropriate methods.

Pros: Inclusive! And it enables teachers to tailor their styles to student needs and appropriate subject matter.

Cons: Hybrid style runs the risk of trying to present too many things to all students, prompting teachers to spread themselves too thin and dilute learning.

(Adapted from *education. cu-portland. edu*)

Why Chinese Students Choose to Study Abroad

Although the higher education sector in China is going from strength to strength, still, many Chinese students are heading overseas to study. In fact, China continues to be one of the leading countries sending students to study abroad and this demand for overseas education remains strong.

Here are the top nine reasons why Chinese students are choosing to head overseas for their university education.

Enriched experience

The majority of Chinese students decide to study abroad to develop a better understanding of other cultures and to gain a global mindset.

The opportunity to experience the different languages, cuisines and customs is exciting. By absorbing a new cultural environment and learning from a different educational system, many students feel they have a more enriched experience than if they had studied in their home country.

Meet a diverse range of people

Going overseas to study unlocks the opportunity to make friends with people from all around the world. You study, live and travel with a diverse range of people — creating an international network of life-long friends. These relationships and memories are one of the biggest positives to studying abroad.

Future employment prospects

Chinese students have rated future employment prospects as one of their top reasons to study overseas. Among Chinese students and their parents, there is a strong belief that overseas education will enhance job prospects and career development. In recent years, we have seen a trend towards students working in the studying country for some time before heading back to their home country.

Language skills

By studying in an English-speaking country, students can learn and improve their language skills. They can quickly pick up the new language and improve their grammar and spelling much faster than if they had stayed in China.

Avoid entrance exam in China for higher education

The entrance exam in China (Gaokao) is one of the most stressful periods of time for both Chinese students and their parents. In China, it is the most important exam for all high school graduates looking to get an undergraduate education. Therefore it comes as no surprise that many parents rank avoidance of entrance exam as a big reason to study abroad. In fact, many parents view it as a good opportunity for their kids to escape this intense and fierce competition.

Preparation for immigration and working abroad

Some students have the intention to eventually move to a foreign country. However, because of the strict application process and eligibility requirements, they choose to study abroad so that they can prepare for the immigration process beforehand. When we look at education levels and fields of study most sought by Chinese students, the master's degree comes on top, closely followed by the bachelor's degree. Business is the most popular field of study for Chinese students.

Influenced by their friends

There are a small number of students that choose to study in a foreign country because of the influence from their friends. This isn't always the main factor but is one of the reasons that can persuade a student towards going abroad.

Better environment

Chinese students also believe that studying overseas gives them a better educational environment. This is because overseas schools offer a more flexible learning environment, with a greater focus on improving the student's soft skills, such as leadership, teamwork and decision-making.

Requested by parents

Lastly, a small minority of students go abroad to study simply because their parents requested it. Parents have a large influence on their children in Chinese culture, so many students may feel that by studying abroad they are adhering to their parents' wishes and upholding family honor.

(Adapted from *timeshighereducation.com*)

B2. Passage Reading

B2.1 Different Teaching Styles

The following two passages focus on different styles of education east and west. Read and give your opinions according to the questions. Try to seek diverse perspectives and don't confine yourself to the reference words and expressions given.

Passage One

Chinese Teaching Methods Lead to Educational Success

Alice Gottesman and Graeme Paton

China is known for having educational success. 70 United Kingdom-based teachers were sent to Shanghai in 2014 to study Chinese teaching methods. Surprised with what they found, they returned to the U. K. and reported China's success in the classroom comes from the "**chalk and talk**" approach — a teaching method the West has been moving away from.

The "chalk and talk" approach is an example of **direct instruction**; it is when the teacher remains at the front of the classroom, directing learning, **controlling classroom activities** and **ensuring a disciplined environment.** This method has contributed to China's great success in international tests such as the Program for International Student Assessment (PISA), Trends in International Mathematics and Science Study (TIMSS) and Progress in International Reading Literacy Study (PIRLS).

Despite the technique's proven success, the West **strayed from** direct instruction in the late 1960s and early 1970s. In an attempt to improve teaching methods, it developed what is referred to as **discovery learning**: basing learning on children's interests, giving them more control over classroom activities and **eliminating mental arithmetic.**

Jun Yang-Williams, a teacher in English schools who previously taught in China, said, "It seems... that British schools have almost **dismissed the 'teacher-led' teaching style....** Although the 'teacher-led' pedagogy is seen as passive, it does not necessarily **jeopardize learning outcomes.** Students are in fact more **proactive** and more responsible for their learning."

These supposedly **innovative techniques** were proven to do the opposite of what the West was trying to accomplish. A recent study of classrooms in the U. K. and China found increasing evidence that new-age teaching methods lead to **under-performance.**

Professor David Reynolds of Southampton University and postgraduate research student Zhenzhen Miao also conducted a test in 2014 on 562 students aged 9 and 10 from

Southampton in the U. K. and from Nanjing in China using math tests from TIMSS. The average Chinese score was 83 percent, whereas the average English score was just 56 percent.

By **establishing the basics** and **spending more time** on teacher-led style, Chinese teaching methods lead to educational success. Teachers constantly ask and answer questions, invite students to **demonstrate solutions on the board** and **quiz students about their thinking**. The classroom is involved, but **driven by the teacher** rather than the students.

Even with teacher-driven classrooms, students **are content with** Chinese teaching methods. According to the 2012 PISA survey, 85 percent of Shanghai's students agreed that they "feel happy at school"— a percentage much higher than the Organization for Economic Cooperation and Development (OECD) average.

Perhaps the West will consider reintroducing direct instruction to its teaching methods.

Schools should **adopt Chinese-style tactics** such as evening classes and **a purge on time-wasting** between lessons to **raise standards** in key subjects, according to the Education Minister Elizabeth Truss.

Teachers need to "learn from the Asian tigers" to ensure pupils **catch up with their peers** in top-performing countries, and schools need to be "much more ambitious" to stop children **slipping behind** in disciplines such as maths and science. She said in a speech.

A study last month by the Organization for Economic Co-operation and Development found that schoolchildren had **stagnated** in recent years as those in China, Singapore, Hong Kong, South Korea and Japan **surge ahead**.

Addressing the Oxford Conference in Education on Friday, Mrs Truss said the gulf was most damaging in maths, which is seen as vital to help drive forward the economy. "We need to be much more ambitious," she said. "Our ambition must be to **out-educate** the rest of the world. Until we agree that doing well is an unequivocally good thing, and that it is attainable by all, we will continue to waste talent."

A report found that — over the last year — a number of tactics had been adopted from Chinese schools.

This included restructuring the school day to **cut down on "slack time"**— wasted minutes between lessons and during registration — to create an additional 30-minute "enrichment session".

Teachers could use this **booster lesson** to **squeeze in** additional "fast learning activities" for pupils in maths, the report said.

Other schools introduced a series of hour-long after-school maths classes — in place of homework — to make sure pupils use their evening time properly.

The report said additional changes included advanced maths topics for younger primary school pupils, a focus on mental arithmetic and more time spent undertaking in-service training for teachers.

New rules — unveiled last year — will give all schools the power to rip up the traditional **school day** and **academic year** to offer **extended teaching.** "Teaching children in high-quality lessons after school means pupils have access to the excellent facilities and teaching available at the school, with clear benefits to children's **attainment.**"

(Adapted from *telegraph.co.uk*; *borgenproject.org*)

Passage Two

Progressive Teaching: Experience over Facts

Robert Kennedy

Progressive education is a reaction to the traditional style of teaching. It's a **pedagogical** movement that **values experience over learning facts** at the expense of understanding what is being taught.

The progressive education philosophy says that educators should teach children how to think rather than **relying on rote memorization.** Advocates argue that the process of **learning by doing** is at the heart of this style of teaching. The concept, known as **experiential learning**, uses **hands-on projects** that allow students to learn by actively engaging in activities that put their knowledge to use.

Progressive education is the best way for students to experience real-world situations, say advocates. For example, the workplace is a **collaborative** environment that requires teamwork, **critical thinking**, **creativity**, and the ability to work independently. Experiential learning, by helping students develop these skills, better prepares them for college and life as productive members of the workplace.

Though progressive education is often looked upon as a modern invention, it actually has deep roots. John Dewey (Oct. 20, 1859-June 1, 1952) was an American philosopher and educator who started the progressive education movement with his influential writings.

Dewey argued that education should not simply involve making students **learn mindless facts** that they would soon forget. He thought that education should be a journey of experiences, building upon each other to help students create and understand new experiences. Teachers in a progressive education system often **sit among students** at a round table designed to **facilitate interaction** between the teacher and students during class.

Dewey also felt that schools at the time tried to create a world **separate from students' lives.** School activities and the life experiences of the students should **be connected**, Dewey believed, or else real learning would be impossible. **Cutting students off from their psychological ties** — society and family would make their learning journeys less meaningful and thereby make learning less memorable.

In traditional education, the teacher **leads the class from the front**, whereas a more progressive teaching model sees the teacher as a **facilitator** who interacts with students and encourages them to think and question the world around them.

Many educational institutions have adopted progressive education, such as The Independent Curriculum Group, a community of schools that says education should include students' "needs, capacities, and voices" as the heart of any program and that learning can be both an end unto itself and **a doorway to discovery and purpose.**

(Adapted from *thoughtco.com*)

Opinion sharing

(a) Summarize the features of Chinese and Western way of education.
(b) How do you comment on your high school education?
(c) Which teacher in high school did you love and respect? What kind of teaching style did he / she adopt?
(d) Which way of teaching do you think is best suited to your personal development, teacher-led or student-centered?
(e) Do you think you have benefited from the Chinese education so far? In which aspects? Please elaborate.

Reference Words and Expressions

absorb	吸收，理解
note-taking	记笔记，随手记
determination	决心
competitive	竞争的，有竞争力的
concentrate	集中，专心于
exam-oriented	应试的
challenging	挑战性的
informality	非正式，不拘礼节
self-management	自我管理
skill-oriented	技能导向的
lengthy lecture	冗长的授课

direct instruction	直接指令,直接教学(法)
core academic subjects	核心学术课程
incredible commitment	难以置信的承诺
immaculate behavior	无可挑剔的行为
interminable day	冗长的一天
be top of the class	名列前茅
be engaged / disengaged with the lessons	参与/不参与到课程中去
variety in learning	多元化学习
narrow/ broad curriculum	狭窄的/广泛的课程
tight schedule	紧张的日程
excel in	在……方面胜过,在……方面很擅长
squeeze in additional lessons	塞进额外的课程
supplemental education tutoring	课外辅导
able students	有能力的学生
deliver a lecture	讲课
speak one's mind	直言不讳
stressed out	紧张的,有压力的
daily routine	日常生活/工作
stifle one's creativity / imagination	扼杀一个人的创造力/想象力
exercise one's organizational skills	锻炼一个人的组织技能
acquire knowledge	获取知识
bear pressure	承受压力
learn actively and creatively	积极和创造性地学习
give priority to	优先考虑……,认为……优先
prove one's worth	证明一个人的价值
potential aptitude	潜在的能力
evaluating criteria	评价标准
harmonious development	和谐发展,协调发展
educational equity	教育公平,教育平等
recognize special talents	识别特殊人才
assist students in varied aspects	在各个方面协助学生
foster learning attitude	培养学习态度
students of caliber and substance	有素质有内涵的学生
cater to students' needs	迎合学生的需要
after-school classes	课外辅导班
high-stake test	非常重要的考试(选拔性升学考试)
all-round development	全面发展
nurture self-reliance	培养自立

Speaking Activities

Dialogue

During the summer holiday, you have an opportunity to visit Princeton University in the U. S. While sitting in on a class, you meet a student there named Marcus. After class, the two of you go for coffee and talk about your learning experience in your own colleges. (You are of the same major.)

Read and discuss

Are Our Kids Tough Enough? Chinese School

According to recent studies, China is home to one of the best education systems in the world, while Britain is trailing a long way behind. In "Are our kids tough enough? Chinese school", five Chinese teachers take over the education of a class of fifty 9-year-old pupils in a Hampshire school. They're here to prove that even a high achieving British school has a lot to learn from their methods. In this unique experiment, the British and Chinese teaching styles are pitched against each other, with both sides tested after four weeks to see who comes out on top. Will the harsh regime of long days and strict discipline produce superior students? Or will the clash of two cultures create chaos in the classroom?

Science teacher Yang Jun (Ms. Yang in the "*Are our kids tough enough? Chinese school?*" series) mulls over her time at Bohunt Academy:

> My teaching timetable was set against a typical Chinese school timetable, starting at 7 a. m. and finishing at 7 p. m. This included the national flag raising ceremony, morning exercise, eye exercises, extended evening self-study sessions, and classroom-cleaning tasks carried out by students. However, this timetable was already a modified and compromised one, as many Chinese students finish their evening revision sessions at 9 p. m. I wondered how my English students would cope with these long school days.
>
> My science lessons took place in a science laboratory, where fifty individual tables and chairs had been positioned in lines and rows. It was a typical Chinese classroom layout but the room was long and narrow. A class of fifty students would sit in this room and I was wondering if students at the back would see my writing as they sat so far away.
>
> I considered my first lesson a success as students were very engaged in observing my demonstrations, taking notes and were well behaved. This is what I would

expect in a Chinese classroom using the "teacher-led" teaching style. It is supposed to be authoritarian and formal, where the teacher stands in front of a class and explains the textbook, and students sit and listen. Students stand up to greet teachers as they walk into the room, and sit quietly afterward taking notes and doing exercises. Unfortunately, my honeymoon period didn't last long.

(Adapted from *open. edu*)

(a) What do you think of Ms. Yang's timetable? Describe your timetable. And how do you think the British students will cope with this typical Chinese school timetable?

(b) Ms. Yang said "*my honeymoon didn't last long.*" Try to imagine what might have happened after the first class that gives Ms. Yang a hard time.

(c) Pair work. You and your partner act as Ms. Yang and a British student in her class. Act out a scene in the classroom, featuring a major conflict between them.

(d) What do you expect the outcome will be? Will the harsh regime of long days and strict discipline produce superior students? Or will the clash of two cultures create chaos in the classroom?

Read and debate

Happy Education

The concept of "happy education", as the Chinese media has termed these policies, first appeared a decade ago, when Shanghai's municipal education authority banned local kindergartens from placing excessive academic demands — such as requiring that students learn 1,000 Chinese characters — on preschoolers. In 2010, a new national education reform and development plan named reducing stress for students in China's "compulsory education" period — from grade one to grade nine — as a key objective.

The policy aimed to relieve the immense academic pressure on China's children. The first 11 months of 2010 had seen 73 primary and middle school students commit suicide, and many educators and psychologists attributed students' mental and physical health issues to overwork. Wang Dinghua, a leading official from the Ministry of Education, said the authority needed to do something to ease the academic burden on children.

(Adapted from *sixthtone. com*)

(a) What do you think of "happy education"? Will it bring good results in students' academic development?

(b) Many Chinese students think that they are under huge academic stress. Do you agree? Do you think stress plays a positive or negative role in the path to academic success? Work in pairs or groups and carry out a debate.

B2.2 Education Online or in Traditional Classrooms

The following two passages focus on education online or in traditional classrooms. Read and give your opinions according to the questions. Try to seek diverse perspectives and don't confine yourself to the reference words and expressions given.

Passage One

Online Education in India

Krunal Sagan

It isn't a secret anymore that the market of online education is growing fast all over the world and India isn't left behind.

India is a country where one could experience total opposite sides of spectrum, on one side you could see people might not have the availability of drinking water but at the same time it is the country with **highest Internet users** in the world. When you mix world's largest young population in a fast-developing country with higher unemployment and **tough competition**, you get students who **embrace any opportunity** that **sets them apart from** competition with open arms. It's hardly a surprise that students in India and other developing world have **heavily adopted online learning** considering the **vast benefits** (such as access to **world class knowledge pools** including Harvard, Stanford, MIT professors, **flexibility in time and pace of learning**, **comfortable learning experience**, **less anxiety**, **customized learning experiences** and teachers can speak to a wider audience, etc.) it offers.

But, India or the world for that matter, hasn't seen drastic change in traditional education system yet. A few years ago, the world was going crazy over how technology was going to **transform higher education** and would replace **physical colleges.** But the current actual scenario couldn't be further from that. According to a University of Pennsylvania study "The Life Cycle of a Million MOOC Users", an average of only five percent of the students in seventeen Coursera classes offered through the University of Pennsylvania actually finished their classes. Other estimated **completion rates** below thirteen percent. And not all the students who completed their courses necessarily passed. Even in Harvard / MIT courses, the course completion rates are low across the board, from 0.8% to 7.5%.

In a five-year-long study of over fifty thousand students taking both online and face-to-face courses, researchers at Troy University found that online classes had higher **failure rates** than traditional classroom courses. Today, universities worldwide have not seen much effect of MOOCs in terms of enrollment or in the tuition fees.

Major drawbacks of the online studies according to Heather Thomas and Kevin Zencak of the Pennsylvania State University are limited communication, easier to ignore, limited teacher instruction and the need for more personal responsibility.

(Adapted from *edtechreview. in*)

Passage Two

Are Online Degrees Worth It?

Brian Martucci

Even as online education is becoming more appreciated and accepted by employers, Jason B. Huett of the University of West Georgia warns in the *Atlanta Journal-Constitution*, "**Online degrees are not all equal.**" A candidate **seeking an online degree** in order to become employed should consider all of the following.

Science, technology, engineering, and math (STEM) are likely to **remain in great demand.** However, many employers prefer a traditional setting for a STEM degree, believing that the experience produces **a better-rounded, better-educated graduate.**

At the same time, many online schools work directly with large employers to **create a curriculum and experience** that these employers would like their new hires to undergo. For example, HCA Healthcare, which owns hundreds of hospitals across the nation, consults with private, not-for-profit Western Governors University to be sure graduates have the skills the company needs. UPS is working with several community colleges to develop online logistics and supply chain programs, and the University of Phoenix is currently **developing online programs** in retail and hospitality management in conjunction with several national employers.

Name recognition and **familiarity** may be the most important factors **in the evaluation of an online degree.** When referring to schools that offer such degrees, reputation is as important to the student as location is to a retailer. Generally speaking, an online degree from **a traditional, accredited university** has more employment value than a degree from **a solely online institution**, even if it's accredited and more difficult to achieve.

Many employers, especially small and medium-sized companies, favor traditional degrees, likely because they're more familiar with them. All things being equal, employers are probably going to judge your education based upon their own familiarity with the institution granting the degree. It is always easier to be hired at companies where other online graduates work than to have to break down the barrier yourself.

Though fortunately views are changing, a degree from a traditional university with **a focus upon classroom instruction** continues to have more value in employers' minds than a degree from an online, accredited institution of learning. In addition, **physically**

attending a school allows the student to **make valuable contacts with peers and instructors** that are likely to **pay future dividends.**

(Adapted from *moneycrashers. com*)

Opinion sharing

(a) What can you derive from the facts in passage one and two?
(b) Without considering financial factors, would you prefer to study online or in traditional classrooms for university education? Give reasons.
(c) MOOC is getting more and more popular; do you think it can revolutionize the way of higher education in China?
(d) If you can make a choice, which courses would you rather take online?
(e) In your opinion, what can the spread of online education do to our education system? List the possible upside and downside.

Reference Words and Expressions

interruption	中断,干扰
procrastinate	耽搁,延迟
self-pacing	自我控速
flexibility	灵活性
off-campus	校外的
commute	通勤

solution to inequality and rising costs	不平等和成本上升的解决办法
large-scale online class	大规模的网络课堂
two-tiered education system	双重教育体系
hands-on experience	实践经验，实际动手经验
lack of access to high quality courses	缺乏接触高质量课程的机会
spread out the work over a period of time	将工作分散在一段时间内
lengthy commute	漫长的通勤
be physically present	现场出席
bricks and mortar	实体的,实际存在的
exaggerate / reduce inequality	夸大/减少不平等
raise hands and ask questions	举手提问
more/ less contact with students	与学生多/少接触
enduring personal bonds	持久的人际关系
personal connection	人际关系,人事关系
show up	露面,露出,揭露
sense of camaraderie	同志般的感情

live lecture in a classroom	在教室里的现场授课
put off until later	推迟到晚些时候
command one's attention	要求某人的注意
connect with each other	相互联系
collaboration among students	学生间的合作
flexible office hours	灵活的办公时间
online whiteboard	在线白板
hit the pause button	按下暂停键
rewind the video	回放视频
clear up confusion	消除困惑
have trouble keeping up with lectures	跟不上讲座的进度
miss key points	错过要点
adjust the pace of learning	调整学习节奏
be held up by questions	被问题困扰
slow the pace as much as needed	尽可能放慢速度
watch the lectures repeatedly	反复观看讲座
flexible hours	弹性工作时间
scheduling problems	时间安排问题
online chat rooms	网络聊天室
valuable internship opportunities	有价值的实习机会
participate in cutting edge research	参与前沿研究
maintain a fluid and solid learning process	保持流畅稳定的学习过程

Speaking Activities

Individual talk

(a) Have you ever taken any online courses? Talk about one of the classes that you enjoyed and one that you disliked.

(b) Can you analyze the reasons why you like the class from all possible perspectives?

(c) Give an all-around analysis of the reasons why you dislike the class.

Group work: classroom design

(a) Work in groups. Design an online course that you think will be very useful and popular among Chinese college students. Then explain the principles you use to judge whether an online course is successful.

(b) Work in groups. Design a traditional course in the classroom. Demonstrate your way of teaching and try to get as many students as possible to like your lecture.

Read and discuss

Education Continues via Online Platforms during Disease Outbreak

Online education, like online tests, live-streaming courses and learning resources, enriched students' winter vacation during the coronavirus outbreak in China, as the Ministry of Education issued a notice earlier to postpone the 2020 spring semester in an attempt to stop the epidemic before it gets on campus, and to ensure the safety and health of teachers and students, a report issued Monday by *People's Daily* said.

(Adapted from *chinadaily. com. cn*)

(a) There were different opinions about adopting online education during the special period of time. What was your response when you heard the news?

(b) How was the online learning at home? Was it effective? When compared to attending school physically, which one is more effective?

(c) If you can alter the situation, what do you propose as a better solution when the new semester was postponed? Why?

B3. Extensive Reading

How to Tell if Online Education Is Right for You

Online education is a growing field that many students are turning to as they pursue undergraduate or graduate degrees. Not sure if you want to earn a degree through a distance learning program? Check out our traits below to see if online education is right for you.

Traits of an online student

Before you decide which traits from our list apply to you, here's a brief breakdown and explanation of some of the traits that can be found in online students. We've ranked the traits based on importance to help give you an idea of which are "must-haves" and which are "nice-to-haves".

Trait	Explanation
1. Have Computer and Internet Access	You can't complete an online degree program if you're not able to get to a computer or log in to the Internet, so easy access is important.

Continued

Trait	Explanation
2. Self-motivator	As an online student, you need to be able to motivate yourself to get your work done since you might not have all of the constant reminders that students in more traditional settings get.
3. Good at Meeting Deadlines	You might have specific deadlines for turning in assignments or posting on a discussion board, so you need to be able to keep track and meet those deadlines so you get credit for your work and participation.
4. Comfortable Participating in Online Discussions	Since many online programs require you to participate in discussion boards, it's important that you're willing to share your thoughts and ideas.
5. Comfortable Working Independently	Online learning means doing things on your own time, so you need to be able to work on your own and without the structure of being in a classroom.
6. Organized	You need to be able to keep your course materials and assignments orderly so that you don't let anything fall through the cracks. You also need to know when things are done, when there are lectures you need to check out and how to make use of resources so that you can get the most out of an online environment.
7. Responsive to Online Communications	Your professors and classmates will communicate with you via email and possibly online chat, so you need to be good about checking for them and responding to them on a regular basis and in a timely manner.
8. Good at Planning Ahead	You need to have a good grasp on all of your personal and professional commitments so that you can properly plan fitting in your educational commitments.
9. Enjoy Using the Computer	Since online students spend a lot of time on their computers in order to listen to lectures, communicate with others and complete assignments, it's important that you like using a computer and don't see it as your arch nemesis.
10. Prefer Flexible Scheduling Options	Many online students are juggling a lot of commitments, like a career and family, so flexible scheduling is important to them.

(Adapted from *study. com*)

References

Amy Morin. (2019). Types of Parenting. *Verywellfamily*. Retrieved from https://www. verywellfamily. com/types-of-parenting-styles-1095045 on March 19th, 2021.

Lac Su. (2011). "Tiger Mothers" Leave Lifelong Scars. *CNN*. Retrieved from http://edition. cnn. com/2011/OPINION/01/20/lac. su. tiger. mother. scars/index. html on March 19th, 2021.

Claire C. Miller and Jonah E. Bromwich. (2019). How Parents Are Robbing Their Children of Adulthood. *New York Times*. Retrieved from www. nytimes. com/2019/03/16/style/snowplow-parenting-scandal. html on March 19th, 2021.

Mane Grigoryan. (2021). College Admissions Scandal. *Marca*. Retrieved from https://www. marca. com/en/lifestyle/2021/03/18/60533e47e2704eaa358b459b. html on March 19th, 2021.

Father Absence. *All4 kinds*. Retrieved from https://www. all4kids. org/2018/06/07/a-fathers-impact-on-child-development/ on March 19th, 2021.

Sara Horn. (2017). A Mother's Influence. *Focus on the Family*. Retrieved from https://www. focusonthefamily. com/parenting/a-mothers-influence/ on March 19th, 2021.

Five Tips for Successful Parenting. *Parenting Code*. Retrieved from https://www. parentingcode. com/blog/5-tips-for-successful-parenting on March 19th, 2021.

Why Is Education Crucial? *University of People*. Retrieved from https://www. uopeople. edu/blog/10-reasons-why-is-education-important/ on March 19th, 2021.

Staff Writer. (2020). Introduction: Why Is College Education So Important? *Reference*. Retrieved from https://www. reference. com/world-view/college-education-important-265d13adeb4868ef on March 19th, 2021.

Why Is College Education So Important? *Study. com*. Retrieved from https://study. com/education. html on March 19th, 2021.

Eric Gill. (2020). Different Teaching Styles. *Resilient Educator*. Retrieved from https://resilienteducator. com/classroom-resources/5-types-of-classroom-teaching-styles/ on March 19th, 2021.

Dandan Cheng. (2018). Why Chinese Students Choose to Study Abroad. *Times Higher Education*. Retrieved from https://www. timeshighereducation. com/student/advice/nine-reasons-why-chinese-students-choose-study-abroad on March 19th, 2021.

Alice Gottesman. (2016). Chinese Teaching Methods Lead to Educational Success. *The Borgen Project*. Retrieved from https://borgenproject. org/chinese-teaching-methods-success/ on March 19th, 2021.

Graeme Paton. (2014). Chinese Teaching Methods Lead to Educational Success. *Telegraph*. Retrieved from https://www. telegraph. co. uk/education/educationnews/

10549462/Schools-should-adopt-Chinese-style-lessons-says-minister. html on March 19th, 2021.

Robert Kennedy. (2019). Progressive Teaching: Experience over Facts. *ThoughtCo.* Retrieved from https://www. thoughtco. com/progressive-education-how-children-learn-today-2774713 on March 19th, 2021.

Are Our Kids Tough Enough? Chinese School and Share Your Opinions. *OpenLearn.* Retrieved from https://www. open. edu/openlearn/tv-radio-events/tv/are-our-kids-tough-enough-chinese-school on March 19th, 2021.

Dandan Ni. (2017). Happy Education. *Sixth Tone*. Retrieved from http://www. sixthtone. com/news/1807/why-has-% 20happy-education% 20-produced-unhappy-students on March 19th, 2021.

Krunal Sagan. (2017). Online Education in India. *EdTechReview*. Retrieved from https:// edtechreview. in/trends-insights/insights/2823-online-vs-offline-education-winner-private-tutors on March 19th, 2021.

Brian Martucci. (2020). Are Online Degrees Worth It? *Money Crashers*. Retrieved from https://www. moneycrashers. com/online-degrees-worth-it/ on March 19th, 2021.

Junwei Wang. (2020). Education Continues via Online Platforms during Disease Outbreak. *China Daily*. Retrieved from http://www. chinadaily. com. cn/a/202002/03/WS5e37e3d4a3101282172747ea. html on March 19th, 2021.

How to Tell if Online Education Is Right for You. *Study. com*. Retrieved from https://study. com/articles/How_to_Tell_if_Online_Education_is_Right_for_You. html on March 19th, 2021.

Unit 2 Psychology

Part A Happiness

A1. Introduction

Different Types of Happiness

What is HAPPINESS? What is the definition of happiness? Can happiness be defined?

In an article on Forbes. com, George Bradt writes that a survey of Harvard's class of 1980 concluded that, "Happiness comes from choosing to be happy with whatever you do, strengthening your closest relationships and taking care of yourself physically, financially and emotionally." The same article says that 2015 Survey by Grant and Glueck Studies shows:

(1) 67% of those extremely happy said the happiest period of their lives is now.
(2) 77% of those extremely happy said the state of their relationship was either the "greatest" or "very good".
(3) 93% of those extremely happy said they are in excellent or very good health.

Merriam Webster defines happiness as, "A state of well-being and contentment."

Vocabulary. com says, "Happiness is that feeling that comes over you when you know life is good and you can't help but smile. It's the opposite of sadness."

The human pursuit of happiness is one of the most common human searches, but it tends to be an elusive goal as well. Luckily for us, the experience of "happiness" can actually take many forms and result from a variety of behaviors and life circumstances. Research can now point us to concrete ways that we can find or develop these various forms of happiness in our lives.

Joy

The feeling of joy comes from losing yourself in the present moment and appreciating what you have. It's fleeting in that it can sneak up on you and sometimes can disappear if you try to analyze it too much. It can also be found in many things if you have the right attitude and perspective, so it's a relatively accessible form of happiness to seek.

The easiest way to find joy is to engage in activities you know usually bring you joy. This can be anything from yoga to amusement parks to your favorite music. It's also important to try some new things to find novel avenues of joy.

Excitement

Though it can last longer than joy, this emotion is still somewhat fleeting — it dissipates rather quickly and can turn into ennui. However, it can be a motivating factor. Excitement about a new job, for example, can motivate you to work harder, and excitement about a new relationship can motivate you to put more effort into working through difficulties.

Excitement can also help you to get through jitters.

If you tell yourself you are excited rather than anxious or nervous, studies have found, you can channel that potentially uncomfortable energy into more constructive activity.

Excitement can also extend the positive feelings you get from an activity. If you focus on your excited feelings of anticipation, the fun of a vacation can extend into the days and weeks before you even leave. Excitement isn't too difficult to come by, either, so this is an easy one to pursue. Take on new challenges. Keep a bucket list. Let yourself revel in anticipation when you have something big coming up.

Gratitude

Gratitude can disappear if you don't actively focus on it, but it's also an important form of happiness. Those who feel gratitude on a regular basis tend to be happier and healthier than those who are less prone to these feelings, according to research.

Further, gratitude is very simple to cultivate. You can use a gratitude journal, loving-kindness meditation, or even simply tell people in your life that you appreciate them, and do it often. Cultivating these feelings of gratitude has been shown to ward off feelings of depression, among other things. It may be less obvious, but this type of happiness can be brought to mind again and again.

Pride

While smug or competitive pride can be a negative thing, feelings of pride in your accomplishments can be a form of gratitude turned inward and are a great form of happiness to indulge in. You can take pride in your work and your family, your home and yourself, and in anything you put effort, care, and love into.

You can cultivate a healthy sense of pride by including personal accomplishments in your gratitude journal or keeping a list of "wins" at the end of each day. This isn't the same as bragging or being "full of yourself" — you're not saying that you're better than others because of your accomplishments, but that you're a better form of yourself, and you're appreciating this fact.

Optimism

Studies also connect optimism with greater outcomes in life. Optimists tend to focus on possibilities and have a combination of gratitude and pride. They're grateful for all of the possibilities life presents, proud of their abilities to harness these resources, and have a strong belief in themselves and their ability to make their attempts at whatever goals they pursue success.

Optimists, when faced with disappointment, tend to minimize it, pinpoint how they can do better next time, and see mitigating factors that led to their negative outcomes. When they succeed, they give themselves credit and take it as a sign of better things to come. Optimism tends to be an overall way of being, so it's less fleeting than other forms of happiness.

(Adapted from *successconsciousness.com*; *verywellmind.com*)

A2. Passage Reading

A2.1 Money and Happiness

The following two passages focus on different extremes of money-happiness issue. Read and give your opinions according to the questions. Try to seek diverse perspectives and don't confine yourself to the reference words and expressions given.

Passage One

Can Money Buy Happiness?

Karen Hopkin

Most people think money can't buy happiness. But according to a recent study, there may be a **loophole**. A team of researchers finds that **shelling out for** services that save time can bring greater feelings of life satisfaction than, say, simply buying more stuff. The results appear in the *Proceedings of the National Academy of Sciences*.

It's safe to say that most of us often feel **crunched** for time. So much so that we are experiencing what Ashley Whillans of the Harvard Business School, the lead author of the study, describes as a **"time famine"**. And like any famine, this chronic lack of time **takes its toll on** our health.

"When we feel like our to-do lists are longer than the hours that we have in the day to complete them, we can feel as if our life is **spiraling** out of control, thereby **undermining** our personal well-being."

Well, if time is money, Whillans and her team wondered whether money that's used to buy time could offer some relief, like paying someone else to clean the house, **mow the lawn**, or deliver the groceries.

To find out, the researchers asked more than 6,000 people from the U. S., Canada, Denmark, and the Netherlands to rate their overall satisfaction with life, and to estimate how much money they **lay out** each month to **outsource** unenjoyable daily tasks or otherwise purchase some time off.

And they found that respondents who willingly **swap funds** for free time also report feeling more content — **regardless of** their income or how many hours they work each week.

To **follow up**, the researchers conducted a smaller experiment in which they gave volunteers forty bucks to buy a little something for themselves. The same participants got another forty dollars that they were told to spend on something that would save them time. And again, buying time was more likely to **elevate mood and alleviate anxiety**.

These findings may be hard for some people to, well, buy:
"Even in a sample of 850 millionaires, just over half of our respondents spent money to buy themselves time. These findings link to a broader literature suggesting that we do not always spend money in ways that promote happiness."

Even when we should know better:
"Personally I know that when I recently moved to a new city I had a lot of **errands** to run. I had to let my own data convince me that buying time would make my life easier, less stressful and happier."

(Adapted from *scientificamerican.com*)

Passage Two

Money Can't Guarantee Happiness

David G. Myers

Does money buy happiness? No. Ah, but would a little more money make us a little happier? Many of us **smirk** and nod. There is, we believe, some connection between **fiscal fitness** and feeling fantastic. Most of us would say that, yes, we would like to be rich. Three in four American collegians now consider it "very important" or "essential" that they become "very **well off** financially". Money matters.

Well, are rich people happier? Researchers have found that in poor countries, such as Bangladesh, being relatively well off does make for greater well-being. We need food, rest, shelter and social contact.

But a surprising fact of life is that in countries where nearly everyone can afford life's necessities, **increasing affluence** matters surprisingly little. The correlation between income and happiness is "surprisingly weak", observed University of Michigan researcher Ronald Inglehart in one 16-nation study of 170,000 people. Once becoming comfortable, more money provides diminishing returns. The second piece of pie, or the second $100,000, never tastes as good as the first.

Even lottery winners and the Forbes' 100 wealthiest Americans have expressed only slightly greater happiness than the average American. **Making it big** brings temporary joy. But in the long run wealth is like health: its **utter absence** can **breed misery**, but having it doesn't guarantee happiness. Happiness seems less a matter of getting what we want than of wanting what we have.

Has our happiness **floated upward** with the rising economic tide? Are we happier today than in 1940s, when two out of five homes lacked a shower or tub, when heat often meant feeding wood or coal into a furnace, and when 35 percent of homes had no toilet?

Actually, we are not. Since 1957, the number of Americans who say they are "very happy" has declined from 35 to 32 percent. Meanwhile, the divorce rate has **doubled**, the teen suicide rate has nearly **tripled**, the **violent crime rate** has nearly **quadrupled** (even after the recent decline), and more people than ever (especially teens and young adults) are depressed.

I call this **soaring wealth and shrinking spirit** "the American **paradox**". More than ever, we have big houses and broken homes, high incomes and low morale, secured rights and diminished civility. We excel at making a living but often fail at making a life. We celebrate our **prosperity** but **yearn for purpose**. We cherish our freedom but **long for** connection. **In an age of plenty**, we feel **spiritual hunger**.

(Adapted from *davidmyers.org*)

Opinion sharing

(a) What is happiness in your mind? State your reasons.
(b) Do you agree that "Money can buy happiness"?
(c) Share some powerful points or cases that prove "Money can't buy happiness".
(d) Some people deeply believe that wealth is the precondition of marital happiness. Do you think so, why?

(e) Imagine that you do not resist marrying someone in poverty, but will you allow your daughter to hold the same marital value? Why?

Reference Words and Expressions

contentment	满足,满意
idealist	理想主义者
materialist	物质主义者
priceless	无价的,极贵重的
invaluable	无价的,非常贵重的
fulfillment	履行,实行,满足感
gratification	满意,满足
buffer	缓冲
virtue	美德,优点
resilience	恢复力,弹力
frustration	挫折
hedonia	快感
eudaimonia	幸福
acquaintance	熟人,相识
inalienable	不可分割的,不可剥夺的
unaffordable	买不起的,高价的
booming	繁荣的,飞速发展的
tuition	学费,讲授

medical bill	医疗费用
duty to support parents and raise kids	赡养父母和抚养孩子的责任
bank loan	银行贷款
pay a mortgage	支付抵押贷款
pay off the debt	还清债务
run up a bill	欠账
rip someone off	欺诈,敲竹杠
the down payment on a house	房子首付
squirrel away some money for future	为将来存钱
splash out a big amount of cash	挥霍一大笔钱
pursuit of happiness	追求幸福
bucket list	遗愿清单
gratitude journal	感恩日记
positive psychology	积极心理学
authentic happiness	真实的快乐

spiritual life	精神生活
leisure time	休闲时间
psychological well-being	心理幸福感
face-to-face contact	当面接触
exercise your altruism	锻炼你的利他主义
prosocial behavior	亲社会行为
emotional health	情绪健康
balance of emotions	情绪平衡
constant euphoria	持续的兴奋
commitment and participation	承诺和参与
positive perceptions	积极的认知
health and longevity	健康与长寿
regular physical exercise	定期体育锻炼
improve mood	改善情绪
community activities	社区活动
Money talks.	有钱能使鬼推磨。

Speaking Activities

Individual talk

Many parents use material reward to motivate kids' school performance, but some argue that spiritual award works better. What will you do to motivate kids aged below 12, if you were the parents? Conduct a 2-minute individual talk.

Read and discuss

China Luxury

China delivered more than half the global growth in luxury spending from 2012 to 2018, and is expected to deliver 65 percent of the world's additional spending heading into 2025, according to research based on Union Pay transaction data for the 2019 McKinsey China Luxury Report. In 2018, Chinese consumers at home and abroad spent 770 billion RMB ($115 billion) on luxury items, equivalent to a third of the global spend, with each luxury-consuming household spending an average of 80,000 RMB per year.

(Adapted from *mckinsey.com*)

(a) According to the report, do you think Chinese attach too much importance to material happiness? What made this happen? Share your opinions.

(b) Since money can't buy happiness, why so many people pursue luxury?

(c) Summarize students' viewpoints.

Read and discuss

How to Find Happiness in Your Life?

Are you on a quest to find happiness? While happiness might be elusive or out of your reach at times, which doesn't make it an impossible journey or goal to achieve. On the contrary, happiness could be waiting for you around the next corner if you just hang on. Or, it might be even simpler than that. Happiness might have been with you all along — you just may not have taken the time to realize it was much less complicated than you once believed. You probably know it's not about driving the newest car or having the latest gadget.

(Adapted from *verywellmind.com*)

(a) But what is it that really drives happiness?
(b) In what kinds of circumstances will you obtain authentic happiness?

A2.2 What Actually Brings Us Happiness?

The following two passages focus on the origins of happiness. Read and give your opinions according to the questions. Try to seek diverse perspectives and don't confine yourself to the reference words and expressions given.

Passage One

Does Happiness Come from Process?

Gilbert Ross

I recently **looked back at** the last two years of my life and **contemplated** the lessons I've learned. I wasn't bored, wasn't **in search for** myself, and I wasn't **reeling** after a defeat; I simply wanted to improve and **reflect**. I think this is important — to appreciate our wins, losses, new passions, insights, etc. Not reflecting on our lives and experiences is, well, a wasted chance for growth and learning.

At first, I was going to **jot these lessons down** in my diary but then remembered that we are in **the age of** information sharing and collaboration. So I thought that sharing them here will **extend** their meaning and benefit beyond my own personal gain and that's a great thing.

So without further adieu, here are some of the more profound things I've learned recently.

Focus on the process and not the outcome. This thought was beautifully **summed up** by

Srikumar Rao. He explains how we fail because we focus our energies on the outcome (the object or circumstance we desire) rather than the process itself. When a child learns to walk, she never focuses on the outcome but **solely** on the process. Success is then **unthought** but very probable outcome.

Failure is a lead not a **stop sign**. When you hit a wall and things don't turn up the way they were intended, no one is saying to you: "This is where you stop because you failed." If you do, you are reading the wrong information. Failure tells us, "This method and the intended result do not **match**. Try another method."

Rejection is a **booster** not a **downer**. When you get that **metaphorical slap** in the face (or literal one) after your job application, idea, project, invention or proposal has been rejected, don't waste time feeling bad about it. Stop taking it personally; it's not about you. That slap in the face is a **wake-up call** for you to pick up your things and keep on moving. Things get rejected every second. So **stop the fuss and move on!**

Happiness is not the **destination** but the journey. We think that happiness is a result that comes after having acquired or achieved something we don't have. The problem is that we are creating the wrong model in our mind in which we link happiness to something that is still to come. This brings **eternal dissatisfaction** not happiness. Happiness is when we accept and enjoy everything as it is. It's about stepping back and enjoying the ride rather than expecting it at your destination point.

Mind vs. Heart = **Turbulence**, Mind + Heart = Wisdom. Let your heart talk more; it's wiser than you think. You can be as knowledgeable and clever as one can be but if your mind is **out of sync** with your heart, you are losing a lot of energy in internal conflict. Wisdom is really having reached a stage where you balance all your knowledge and intellect with your heart, purely and simply.

If you want to be creative, stop trying to create. Creativity is to understand that sometimes you are not the creator but only the **medium** of a **transcendent** creative force, bigger than you or me. This is something I have written about in the past where I compared the creative process to the Yin & Yang duality. It has generative side — the brainstorming & playing with concepts. This takes action and effort. But there is also the **receptive** part which we very often forget. This is **passive** and **intuitive**, **entailing** no action but plain receptivity. If you stop at the generative part of the process, you will have an incomplete creative cycle, and the more you try, the more incomplete it is. So stop trying.

Gratitude is the energy-drink of the soul. Say thank you to the universe every morning. Appreciation and gratitude are instant soul-lifters not as **angst**, **contempt** and **disdain**, which **weigh you down** and **make you dull**. Try it out. Be thankful to at least one thing in your day. It will **nudge** you into appreciating the **delicate equilibrium** of life with more depth and perspective.

(Adapted from *dumblittleman. com*)

Passage Two

Purposeful Life Brings Happiness

Yasemin Saplakoglu

Does your life have purpose? The answer could affect how long you live. And we do believe that happy people live longer.

Having a strong purpose in life may bring not only mental health, but also **physical benefits.**

A new study suggests that **purposeful** living **is linked to** decreased risk of early death in those older than age 50. The new results were published on Thursday (May 23) in the journal *JAMA Network Open*.

A group of researchers at the University of Michigan analyzed data from nearly 7,000 people older than 50 who were enrolled in a national study that began in 1992 and who **filled out** a **psychological questionnaire** in 2006.

Participants were asked to rank how strongly they felt about statements such as "I enjoy making plans for the future and working to make them a reality" and "my daily activities often seem **trivial** and unimportant to me"; these people were then given a "life purpose score".

The researchers then compared these scores with **mortality rates** of the participants over the next five years. During that time, 776 of the participants died.

Participants with the lowest life-purpose scores were more than twice as likely to die **during the follow-up period**, compared with participants with the highest life-purpose scores, the study found. In particular, those with lower life-purpose scores were more likely to die from heart or blood conditions.

The findings held even after the researchers **took into account** certain factors that could affect people's sense of life purpose or their risk of death, such as whether the participants had depression.

"There seems to be no **downside** to improving one's life purpose, and there may be benefits," said lead author Aliya Alimujiang, a doctoral student at the University of Michigan School of Public Health. "Previous research has suggested that volunteering and **meditation** may improve **psychological well-being.**"

The next step for this research will be to determine if interventions designed to increase life purpose really work, and if increasing life purpose leads to good health outcomes such as improved quality of life, she added.

According to the researchers, there are several possible reasons why having a life purpose might **extend life span.**

Past studies have shown that stronger happiness, including purposeful living, decreased the activation of **genes** that **trigger inflammation** in the body. Inflammation, in turn, has been previously linked with an increase in risk of early death, according to the study.

Yet another study found that a stronger purpose in life was linked to lower levels of the **"stress hormone"** cortisol and lower levels of inflammatory **molecules** in the body. But no studies have directly measured such molecules or biomarkers and related them to health outcomes or mortality.

One limitation of the study is that the researchers couldn't exclude the possibility of **"reverse causality"** among participants with a **chronic** or **life-threatening** illness. In other words, the chronic or life-threatening illness could have been driving people to have a lower purpose in life.

In a follow-up analysis, when the researchers excluded people who had a chronic or life-threatening illness, their results still held true, but there was a higher likelihood that these results could have been due to chance, the authors noted.

(Adapted from *livescience.com*)

Opinion sharing

(a) What are the advantages and disadvantages of being process-oriented?
(b) When do we have to be process-oriented or result-oriented? Share your reasons or stories.
(c) How will you define "purposeful living"? Will you link your happiness to purposeful living? Why?
(d) Some people deeply believe that it is tiring to live a social life with clear purposes. Do you agree? Why?
(e) In addition to the biological reasons mentioned above, why do you think people who live a purposeful life live longer?

Reference Words and Expressions

outperform	胜过,做得比……好
capacity	能力,容量
competent	胜任的,有能力的

competitive	竞争的,有竞争力的
complement	补充,补足
vision	视觉,愿景
ambition	雄心,野心
destination	目的地,终点
perseverance	耐性,毅力
failure	失败
realistic	现实的
mundane	世俗的,平凡的
mediocre	普通的,平庸的
deadline	最终期限
schedule	时间表,时刻表

pursue intrinsic goals	追求内在目标
extrinsic goals	外在目标
achievement goal orientation	成就目标导向
mastery goal orientation	掌握目标导向
have the ability to do something	有能力做某事
career plan	职业规划
mental clarity	头脑清晰
life expectancy	预期寿命,平均寿命
life span	寿命;使用期限
self-discipline	自律
in pursuit of	寻求,追求
persist in	坚持
persevere in	坚持
bottom line	底线,最低限度

Speaking Activities

Brainstorm

Suppose that happiness is composed of the following ingredients: a loyal marriage, endurable friendship, a promising career, good education, large fortune, physical health, family love, perfect appearance, inner peace, high EQ, etc. If you have to take three things off the list above, how will you select? Brainstorm and tell your choice, and state why.

Individual speech

Some people believe that we can't tell what true happiness is unless we approach the end of life. Do you support this viewpoint? If you have one month left in this world, what will you put in your will list?

Discussion

Some people hold the view that "if you are not happy, you are flawed". If happiness is associated with flaw, how would you interpret their relationship? Conduct a discussion, and summarize the viewpoints of your group.

Debate

To be a small fish in a big pond or the other way round? Every college graduate faces this question when he / she starts his / her career. A large number of college graduates prefer to stay in big cities. But others want to stay in small towns because they can be a big fish in a small pond.

Topic for debate: Want to be a small fish in a big pond or a big fish in a small pond?

A3. Extensive Reading

Do a Country's Inhabitants Get Happier as It Gets Richer?

Most governments seem to believe so, giving their relentless focus on increasing GDP year by year.

Reliably, long-term evidence linking wealth and happiness is, however, lacking. And measuring well-being is itself fraught with problems, since it often relies on surveys that ask participants to assess their own levels of happiness subjectively.

Daniel Sgroi of the University of Warwick and Eugenio Proto of the University of Glasgow, both in Britain, think, nevertheless, that they have an answer. By examining millions of books and newspaper articles published since 1820 in four countries (America, Britain, Germany and Italy), they have developed what they hope is an objective measure of each place's historical happiness.

And their answer is that wealth does bring happiness, but some other things bring more of it.

Previous research has shown that people's underlying levels of happiness are reflected in what they say or write. Dr. Sgroi and Dr. Proto therefore consulted newspaper archives and so on, a collection of more than 8m titles that constitute around 6% of all books physically published. They searched these texts for words that had been assigned a psychological "valence"— a value representing how emotionally positive or negative a word is — while controlling for the changing meanings of words such as "gay" and "awful" (which once most commonly meant "to inspire awe").

The result is the National Valence Index, published this week in Nature Human Behavior. Placed alongside the timeline of history, the valence indices for the places under study show how changes in national happiness reflect important events. In Britain, for example, happiness fell sharply during the two world wars. It began to rise again after 1945, peaked in 1950, and then fell gradually, including through the so-called Swinging Sixties, until it reached a nadir around 1980.

America's national happiness, too, fell during the world wars. It also fell in the 1860s, during and after the country's civil war.

(Adapted from *gbr. businessreview. global*)

Part B Stress

B1. Introduction

What Is Stress?

A lot of researches have been conducted into stress over the last hundred years. Some of the theories behind it are now settled and accepted; others are still being researched and debated.

During this time, there seems to have been something approaching open warfare between competing theories and definitions: views have been passionately held and aggressively defended.

What complicates this is that intuitively we all feel that we know what stress is, as it is something we have all experienced. A definition should, therefore, be obvious... except that it is not.

Definition of stress

Hans Selye was one of the founding fathers of stress research. His view in his book *The Stress of Life* was that "Stress is not necessarily something bad — it all depends on how you take it. The stress of exhilarating, creative successful work is beneficial, while that of failure, humiliation or infection is detrimental." Selye believed that the biochemical effects of stress would be experienced irrespective of whether the situation was positive or negative.

Since then, a great deal of further researches have been conducted, and ideas have moved on. Stress is now viewed as a "bad thing", with a range of harmful biochemical and long-term effects. These effects have rarely been observed in positive situations.

The most commonly accepted definition of stress (mainly attributed to Richard S. Lazarus in his book *Psychological Stress and the Coping Process*) is that stress is a condition or feeling experienced when a person perceives that "demands exceed the personal and social resources the individual is able to mobilize." In short, it's what we feel when we think we've lost control of events.

This is the main definition used by this section of Mind Tools, although we also recognize that there is an intertwined instinctive stress response to unexpected events. The stress response inside us is, therefore, part instinct and part to do with the way we think.

Eustress and distress

The ideas of "eustress" (good stress) and "distress" (bad stress) were developed by Hans Selye, one of the early researchers on stress. Selye believed that a mild level of stress encouraged animals and people to behave in a more active way, while an excessive level of stress would hamper their performance.

Since then, other people have drawn similar conclusions, substituting the idea of "stress" with the idea of "pressure". Framed in this way, this is an important and valuable idea. With all of its associations of unhappiness and loss of control, real stress is now seen as a bad thing in all circumstances.

The ideas of "eustress" and "distress" are therefore no longer useful. Indeed, they may be harmful in that they may encourage managers to try to motivate subordinates by increasing the amount of unpleasant stress they experience. The error in this approach is clear if you remember that "pressure" is a different thing from "stress".

Measuring stress

Stress can be measured in different ways, but testing usually takes the form of a self-report in which a person rates particular experiences, events, or feelings on a defined scale.

Perhaps the most well-known of these is the SRRS (Social Readjustment Ratings Scale), developed in 1967 by the American psychiatrists Thomas H. Holmes and Richard Rahe. The SRRS lists a number of life events assumed to be stressful, such as moving or the death of a spouse or other close loved one.

Holmes and Rahe assigned a numerical value to each of these events based on the intensity of the stress. The death of a spouse, for example, was rated the most stressful, at 100, whereas a minor violation of the law was assigned a value of 11.

Impact

Broadly speaking, stress can be experienced in two ways, physically and psychologically, but the two are interrelated. For example, research has shown that chronic stress can lead to decreased immune function. This included an increased risk of infection and decreased ability to fight infection or repair tissue.

One study found that stress not only slowed wound healing, it often also led to behaviors that slowed recovery from injury or surgery such as heavy alcohol use or poor self-care.

Physical symptoms

Remember that stress is an individual experience and that symptoms are too. Signs of disease should not be ignored just because you believe they are stress-related. Get serious symptoms checked by your doctor.

Some potential effects of stress include:

- Chest pain
- Pounding heart
- High blood pressure
- Shortness of breath
- Fatigue
- Diminished or increased sex drive
- Muscle aches, such as back and neck pain
- Headaches
- Dizziness
- Clenched jaws and grinding teeth
- Tightness, dryness or a feeling of having lump in your throat
- Indigestion
- Constipation or diarrhea
- Increased perspiration
- Stomach cramps
- Weight gain or loss
- Skin problems

Psychological symptoms

If these effects of stress are interfering with your daily life, consult your doctor for advice on how to find relief. Stress management is essential to well-being and something we should practice every day.

- Sadness
- Depression
- Crying
- Withdrawal or isolation
- Insomnia
- Mood swings
- Worry
- Restless anxiety
- Irritability, anger or decreased anger control
- Overeating or anorexia
- Feelings of insecurity
- Decreased productivity
- Job dissatisfaction
- Changes in close relationships
- Increased smoking
- Increased use of alcohol and drugs

(Adapted from *mindtools.com*; *verywellmind.com*)

B2. Passage Reading

B2.1 Eustress and Distress

The following two passages focus on different extremes of stress issue. Read and give your opinions according to the questions. Try to seek diverse perspectives and don't confine yourself to the reference words and expressions given.

Passage One

Stress Changes the Brain

David DiSalvo

The results of a new brain imaging study may have just answered a big question about how stress changes the brain. Using a combination of genetic editing and brain scanning in mice, researchers found that stress triggers a chemical cascade that radically changes how brain networks communicate, and the results could sharpen our understanding of anxiety disorders in humans.

Breaking down the research

Stress serves an important purpose in preparing us to react to danger. Anything the brain perceives as threatening **triggers** multiple brain networks to **synchronize** and communicate, all in just **a fraction of** a second. With systems humming, we make immediate decisions to survive the threat.

But what **facilitates** all of those brain networks to connect and communicate? That's been a difficult question to answer in the human brain, because doing so would require examining brain function during the split-second window of facing a threat.

Enter our friends the mice to help solve the problem. Researchers followed a trail of previous studies and zeroed in on the neurotransmitter noradrenaline (aka norepinephrine, a chemical that floods the brain during stress) as a likely facilitator of brain-network connectivity. The twist was that they had **genetically manipulated** the **rodents'** brains to allow for **selectively** controlling when noradrenaline was **released** (not possible in human brains). While controlling the chemical **faucet**, they also scanned the mouse brains using FMRI to see what would happen.

And what happened, it turns out, was pretty amazing. The release of noradrenaline "**rewired**" the mouse brains, allowing different brain networks to instantly cross-communicate. But the neurotransmitter wasn't just facilitating communication; it was restructuring neural connections **beyond anyone's expectations**.

"I couldn't believe that we were seeing such strong effects," said the study's first author Valerio Zerbi, a brain imaging specialist from the University of Zurich.

The researchers found the strongest rewired effects in brain areas responsible for processing **sensory stimuli** (**auditory** and **visual**, for example), and in the amygdala, the epicenter of the brain's threat response system.

What does this mean for us?

It's the part about threat response that may hold the most promise for better understanding what stress does to our brains.

Allowing for the fact that this was research in mice, the particular dynamic studied here is probably quite similar between us and our rodent counterparts. If noradrenaline rewires the human brain as it appears to rewire the brains of mice, it's possible the long-term effects of stress are more profound than we've realized.

Previous researches have linked the flood of noradrenaline to changes in brain connectivity, but it seems likely we've **underestimated** the effects, especially in the small but powerful part of our brain sitting at the center of **anxiety disorders**: the amygdala.

At a minimum, this research opens new doors for better understanding how both **acute** and **chronic** stress affects the brain, and could **enlighten** new ways of **deconstructing** anxiety conditions, now the most **prevalent** mental health disorders worldwide.

(Adapted from *forbes. com*)

Passage Two

Some Stress Is Good for People

Robert Sanders

Stress has **measurable** and **significant** physical and mental health impacts (a Yale study found chronic stress can actually shrink your brain), and we hear quite a bit about it, as researchers continue examining its long and short-term influence. They've even **determined** that stress is **contagious**.

We know that chocolate has very real **anti-stress properties**, and that eating a diet high in greens and veggies helps **mitigate** some of the negative physical effects of stress.

But what's not often talked about is that some stress is beneficial. This is not the chronic stress that can hurt you, but the heightened emotional state one feels before speaking in public or writing an important paper. Scientists have found that our abilities peak under moderate levels of stress. And **as long as** it doesn't go on too long, that **short-duration** stress isn't unhealthy.

Short **bursts** of stress can be good for you — but being **perpetually** late all the time probably isn't the best way to accomplish that feeling. A study at the University of

California, Berkeley, found that "Some amounts of stress are good to push you just to the level of **optimal alertness**, behavioral and **cognitive** performance," said Daniela Kaufer, associate professor of integrative biology at the UC Berkeley, in a news release.

Those stress hormones can help animals (and people) adapt to changing environments. For example, we are more likely to remember something if it was accompanied by some level of stress.

"I think **intermittent** stressful events are probably what keep the brain more alert, and you perform better when you are alert," post-doc Elizabeth Kirby told *Forbes* magazine. However, when those stressful events are **continuous**, the opposite occurs and the memory is **impaired**, she said.

The key is keeping stress **limited** to a few moments. When we do, there can be **multiple** benefits, including longevity, as another study revealed.

Researchers found a newly described form of stress called chromatin stress triggering a response in cells that **leads to** a longer life. Although the research was done in yeast, if it has the same response in humans, it could lead to new treatments in the **aging** process.

(Adapted from *news. berkeley. edu*)

Opinion sharing

(a) How do you view the concept of "eustress", can you list some positive stresses in daily life which prove the existence of eustress?
(b) How can eustress motivate one to move on? Share your story or opinion.
(c) As for college entrance examination, some students view it as eustress, but some perceive it to be distress, what makes this happen? Share your opinions.
(d) Distress is something unavoidable in human being's life, how does distress negatively affect you? Share your story.
(e) Many people hold the view that Chinese young generation bears much more pressure than western young generation in many aspects, do you agree? Share your opinions.

Reference Words and Expressions

testy	易怒的,暴躁的
fussy	爱挑剔的,难取悦的
pushy	有进取心的
fatigue	疲劳,疲乏
traumatic	创伤的

exhausted	筋疲力尽的,疲惫不堪的
upsetting	令人心烦意乱的,令人烦恼的
painful	痛苦的
disturbing	令人不安的,烦扰的
unassailable	不容置疑的,无懈可击的
hypertension	高血压,过度紧张
psychiatrist	精神病医生
relaxation	放松
workout	锻炼

heavy / great pressure	巨大的压力
impose / put pressure on someone	对某人施加压力
comfort zone	舒适区
be fraught with stress	充满压力
stress-free life	没有压力的生活
fight-or-flight response	“战或逃”反应
lay stress on	重视,把重点放在
be stressed out	紧张,饱受压力
stress someone out	使某人紧张
press sb to do something	敦促某人做某事
under the gun	压力很大
depression and anxiety	抑郁与焦虑
relieve stress	缓解压力
reduce stress	减轻压力
worn out	疲惫不堪的,耗尽的
push the envelope	尝试全新事物,突破极限
a fast-paced society	快节奏的社会
life rhythm	生活节奏
affect immune cells	影响免疫细胞
affect one's appetite	影响人的食欲
peer pressure	同伴压力
take a significant toll	造成重大损失
social esteem	社会尊重
immune system	免疫系统
increase immunity	增加免疫力
chronic stress	慢性压力,慢性应激,长期不断的压力
diffuse some of the negativity	驱散某些消极情绪
minimize the stress	压力最小化

psychosocial stressors	社会心理压力源
shift your perspective	转变你的观点
exacerbate the level of threat	加剧威胁程度

Speaking Activities

Discussion

Young people grow up and study with peers, and it is common to feel peer pressure any time. How do you perceive peer pressure? Is it beneficial or detrimental? Conduct a group discussion and select a representative to summarize teammates' viewpoints.

Read and discuss

Need a Rival or Not?

In our world, one creature without any rivals is a lifeless creature. If a man lives without rivals, he is bound to be satisfied with the present and will not strive for the better. He would hold back before all difficulties and decline in inaction and laziness. Adverse environment tends to cultivate successful people. Therefore, your rivals are not your opponents or those you grudge. Instead, they are your good friends! In our lives, we need some rivals to "push us into the river", leaving us striving ahead in all difficulties and competitions. In our work, we need some rivals to be picky about us and supervise our work with rigorous requirements and standards. Due to our rivals, we can bring out our potential to the best; due to our rivals, we will continuously promote our capabilities when competing with them!

(Adapted from *xyen.com.cn*)

(a) According to the paragraph above, do you agree that people need rivals to advance? Share your opinions.

(b) Some people view rivals or competitors as eustress, but some take it as distress, how about you? Share your opinions.

(c) Summarize the viewpoints presented.

Brainstorm

Winners Take All

There is no doubt that human society is full of stress. It is inevitable to face fierce competitions during any period of one's life time. "Winners take all" is a famous saying in Psychology, which is also known as Matthew Effect. Some people argue that the rule is unreasonable because most people have to be losers and bear too much pressure, but some hold the view that it makes sense, because the world is run under the rule of survival of the fittest.

(a) How do you view Matthew Effect? Make a comment.

(b) How do you think about the rule of "survival of the fittest"? Does it make sense to you? Why? Share your opinions.

(c) Do you perceive "survival of the fittest" as negative stress? Why? Share your opinions.

B2.2 What Actually Brings Us Stress?

The following two passages focus on the origins of stress and related solutions. Read and give your opinions according to the questions. Try to seek diverse perspectives and don't confine yourself to the reference words and expressions given.

Passage One

Why So Stressed?

Bridget Alex

Ancient organisms likely **evolved** the stress response to better escape from predators. But today's **triggers** include traffic, **deadlines** and first dates. According to a 2018 American Psychological Association survey of more than 3,000 respondents, the top stressors are work, money, the economy and health.

Although everyone faces stress, people react to it differently.

"There's the situation, how we evaluate the situation, and then our skills at handling the situation," says psychologist William Lovallo of the University of Oklahoma. Previous experiences help us **gauge** appropriate responses, so most people improve with age. "A high school student or a college student might not have those coping skills and might let a situation **get out of hand**," he adds.

Most adults have normal stress responses, **calibrated** to give the right **burst of hormones** and bodily changes for a particular stressor. But others **consistently** over- or under-react, which may be a warning sign for physical or mental disorders. To study this, scientists often monitor cortisol or **heart rate fluctuations** throughout the day and during trying tasks.

In some cases, the **intensity** of these responses seems to be set from a young age. Studies have shown that people who experienced childhood **hardships** — including physical punishment, an unstable home and **sexual abuse** — are more likely to have **muted stress** reactions as adults. For example, as part of a study published in 2012,

Lovallo exposed 354 participants to **moderate** stress. People who self-reported early-life **adversity actually had lower heart rates and cortisol levels than other participants. While** the study tasks were **inconsequential**, the individuals' under-reactions suggest their stress response may also have trouble **reviving up** when it really matters, which can be just as unhealthy as an **excessive** response.

Other research has found links between childhood **strife**, **abnormally** low adult stress and substance abuse. Though the biology is not fully understood, it's suggested that early-life neglect or **trauma desensitizes** the body's stress pathways. Even before birth, a child can **inherit** parental stress, either through hormones the developing **fetus** takes in or chemical modifications to the egg or sperm. The phenomenon is well-demonstrated in rats and mice, and some papers have shown the same association in humans. For instance, adult children of Holocaust survivors and babies born to mothers experiencing PTSD from the 9/11 attacks all had low cortisol levels.

(Adapted from *forbes.com*)

Passage Two

How Can We Reduce Our Stress?

Amy Gallo

You constantly hear how bad stress is for you: it's damaging your health, jeopardizing your relationships, and hurting your performance. While these risks are real, recent research is showing that work strain, when managed correctly, can actually have a positive impact on productivity and performance. So how can you take the stress that you thought was killing you and make it constructive?

Why the experts say stress is unavoidable. "We live in a world of ongoing worry, change, and uncertainty. You have to get used to it," says Justin Menkes, an expert in the field of C-suite talent evaluation and the author of *Better Under Pressure: How Great Leaders Bring Out the Best in Themselves and Others*. "Stress is an inevitable part of work and life, but the effect of stress upon us is far from **inevitable**," says Shawn Achor, an expert in positive psychology and the founder of Good Think, Inc.

Both Achor and Menkes agree that altering your approach to stress can **yield** positive effects. "Stress can be good or bad depending on how you use it," says Achor. In fact, how you manage pressures can distinguish you as a leader and give you a career advantage. Here are five principles to follow:

Recognize worry

"When you hear about stress being unhealthy it is so often because people aren't getting to a place where they are seeing worry for what it is: a feeling," says Menkes. The heightened reaction — tension in the body, heart racing — is an indicator of how much you care about the task you are about to do. In fact, according to Menkes, how much stress you feel is directly correlated to the importance of the activity. "If it didn't matter, you wouldn't worry," he says. Once you understand worry as an indicator rather than a symptom of **dysfunction** or a cause for **panic**, you can react to it more **rationally**. Plus, remember that stress is not **unending**. "Feelings by definition are **fleeting**. They feel like they will be eternal but just give it five minutes," says Menkes.

Reframe the stress

Once you've recognized what worry is, you then need to adjust your **mindset**. Achor's research shows that how you view stress **determines** its effect on you. "Our brains work much better at positive than at negative, neutral, or stressed," he says. When you are negative and worried, your brain goes into "fight or flight" mode, which limits your ability to think. If you are positive and concerned, then your brain turns to "broaden and build" thinking which allows you to process more possibilities. Which direction you go in is up to you. "When people have a stress in their life, they can attempt to see it as a challenge, instead of a threat," says Achor. This **mental shift** will allow the feeling to be activating rather than **paralyzing**.

Focus on what you can control

One of the most positive things you can do when faced with worry or anxiety is to remember what you can affect and what you can't. Far too many people spend time feeling bad about things they simply can't change. In Achor's book, *The Happiness Advantage*, he outlines an exercise he calls the Island Experiment. He suggests you write out a list of stresses and put them into two circles, "islands". One island holds the things you can control. The other is for the things you can't. Ignore that second island and choose a single **concrete** action to take in the first. This will begin to solve the stress and move you toward your goal.

Create a network of support

Knowing that you have somebody to turn to can help a lot. "It's important to have that outlet so you know you can **freak the heck out** if you need to," says Menkes. You may not use this option, but it can be comforting to know it's there. Build supportive relationships when you're not stressed. Menkes encourages you to "put in the effort and build the emotional **deposit**" so you can cash it in when and if required. The company you keep also makes a difference. "Surround yourself with people who do not complain or **ruminate upon** things they can't change," says Achor.

Accumulate stress-handling experience

According to Menkes, the best way to learn to handle stress is through practice. "If the body is not used to stress and you experience it, you'll panic and it becomes a **vicious cycle** that needs to be broken," says Menkes. He often sees this in younger people: "They have more intense reactivity than older people. It's not only a function of hormones but it's a function of experience." Don't wait for a **dire** situation to try out these techniques. "Think about ways you can put yourself in non-game-changing, but pressured situations. Pressure and fear are good because it means you are stretching," says Menkes. For example, if public speaking is **nerve-wracking** for you, he suggests you sign up for Toastmasters and try out your skills in a contained setting. Set up experiments in which you feel stress, but can manage it.

Principles to remember

Do:

- Think of stress as an indicator that you care about something, rather than a cause for panic
- Focus on the task, rather than the emotion
- Build relationships so that you have people to turn to in times of stress

Don't:

- Assume your stress is going to last forever
- Worry about things that are out of your control
- Spend time with people who are negative

(Adapted from *hbr.org*)

Opinion sharing

(a) What seems to be your stressors in your life and how do they affect you? Share your life experience.

(b) Is there any stress that you feel like you are unable to manage? After reviewing the two passages, how will you face and handle the terrible stress you are undergoing? Share your opinions.

(c) Do you agree with the saying that whether stress is good or bad is up to your mindset? Share your opinions.

(d) How can we transform stressor to motivator? Share your story or life experience.

(e) Since you have experienced College Entrance Examination in China, you may have personal effective strategies for reducing stress. Share them with your classmates.

Reference Words and Expressions

overwhelming	压倒性的，势不可挡的
despair	绝望
insomnia	失眠
cognitive	认知的，认识的
psychological	心理的，心理学的

weaken	减弱
strengthen	加强
counselor	顾问,法律顾问
resolution	决心
resentful	愤慨的
psychotherapy	心理疗法

feel burnt out	感觉筋疲力尽
freak out	处于极度高涨的情绪(如害怕、兴奋)中
screw up	弄错,弄糟
something is bugging someone	某事困扰某人
mental illness	精神病,精神疾病
commit suicide	自杀
unable to curb one's temper	无法控制自己的脾气
be immune to	对……有免疫力,不受……的影响
inhibit one from doing something	阻止某人做某事
stimulate one to do something	刺激某人做某事
release pressure	释放压力
let off	放出,排放
give vent to	发泄,吐露
under control	处于控制之下
role model	榜样,行为榜样
early intervention	早期干预
slow music	舒缓的音乐
deep breath	深呼吸
choke or survive	窒息或生存
go with the flow	顺其自然,听从大家的意见
sober realist	冷静的现实主义者
be aware of one's shortage	意识到自己的不足
self-appreciation	自我升值
conflict resolution skills	冲突解决技能
bridge the gap	缩小差距
entrenched in	盘踞在
practice assertive communication	练习自信的沟通
insulated from stress	远离压力
quick fix	权宜之计
incorporate into your life	融入你的生活
ride a rollercoaster	坐过山车

self-sabotage thought　　自我破坏的想法
anti-stress solution　　抗应激的解决方案

Speaking Activities

Brainstorm

Talking about stress, both men and women are bearing various stressors in society. In Chinese tradition, a typical man needs to work hard to support his family; a typical woman should go over a lot of physical stress and strain to give birth and nurse kids. But unlike the way in ancient China, modern people have to face much more pressure than ever.

Share your opinions about what stressors men and women have to bear in current society. Your discussion should cover the differences between ancient China and modern China.

Try to make a comparison between male and female, and summarize the viewpoints in your group on the topic, "Who is living a tougher life in China".

Read and discuss

How Can Peer Pressure Affect Us?

Peer pressure can happen when we are influenced to do something we usually would not do, or we are stopped from doing something we would like to do. This may be because we want to be accepted by our peers. A peer can be anyone you look up to or someone who you would think is an equal in age or ability. A peer could be a friend, someone in the community or even someone on TV. You may experience peer pressure as you live up to either the individual's or group's expectations, or follow a particular fashion or trend. Peer pressure may influence us in a number of ways, including our fashion choice, alcohol and other drug use, decision to have a boyfriend / girlfriend, choice of who our friends are and academic performance.

(Adapted from *researchomatic.com*)

(a) How does peer pressure affect young people in daily life? Share your life experience.
(b) Do peers bring you pressure? Are you able to resist it? Why?
(c) In what occasion can peer pressure be positive? Share your opinion.
(d) How does peer pressure affect young people in daily life? Share your life experience.

Debate

Whether to develop a romantic relationship in college has been a controversial topic. Some people believe that it is going to negatively affect individual study, because dating someone definitely consumes a lot of unnecessary time and money which easily impose a lot of stress on students, and this may be especially true to some male students without sufficient pocket money. But other people view boyfriend / girlfriend as a perfect peer who can motivate one to move forward and maintain individual excellence.

Topic for debate: Is developing a romantic relationship in college a good thing or bad thing?

B3. Extensive Reading

Passage One

Can We Resist Peer Pressure?

Brit Garner

Peer pressure is talked about so much that it can seem a little bit like a joke, especially when you're a teenager. But actually, experiencing peer pressure can be so uncomfortable.

Like, did you really want to run that 10k with your super athletic roommates? Maybe not, but they just asked so many times that it was easier to do it than listen to them ask again.

You've probably been told that to resist peer pressure, you should "just say no," but surprise: that doesn't always seem to work. And neither did that DARE program that was everywhere in the '90s.

Psychologically speaking, it totally makes sense that we'd want to give in to social norms — but that doesn't mean it's always a good thing. Thankfully, researchers have come up with some better ideas for resisting peer pressure. So the next time your roommates try to drag you on a run, you'll be prepared. Psychologists believe that we're basically hard-wired to want to feel like we belong.

After all, in our evolutionary past, cooperating with groups was necessary for people to survive. Because of this, social norms have a huge effect on our behavior — especially ones called injunctive norms, which tell us how society thinks we should behave in certain situations. These norms aren't necessarily bad. For example, they're part of why you'd stop at a red light or pay a friend back when they loan you money. But following them can also cause us to act in risky or dangerous ways to fit in.

In an early demonstration of this effect from 1968, 58 male college students were asked to fill out questionnaires about going to an urban school. Then, while they did, the room they were in started to fill with smoke. When the participants were in the room alone, most of them went to get help. But when they were in groups, they were much less likely to, which seems... pretty weird. One possible explanation for this is that the participants looked at other people's behavior to try and figure out how they should respond. If the other people didn't seem stressed by the smoke, they might have decided that it wasn't something they had to worry about.

Now, this was just an experiment, but things like this happen all the time in real life. Like, imagine you're hanging out with your buddies, and someone turns on the worst, most horrible-sounding music you can possibly imagine. Except, you don't say anything, and neither does anybody else. So you're all just sort of politely sitting there, and you might come to the conclusion that your friends actually enjoy this terrible music, and maybe you're the problem.

Psychologists actually have a name for this concept: pluralistic ignorance. It's the idea that a group might feel a certain way, but nobody in the group realizes it because everyone is keeping their true feelings to themselves. Because of this, you might come to think a certain social norm exists — like that smoky rooms are totally normal — even if everybody else is secretly just as uncomfortable with the situation.

Pluralistic ignorance can play a huge role in peer pressure, and psychologists have also suggested it might be a factor in the heavy drinking that often occurs on college campuses.

In a 1993 study at Princeton University, researchers asked 132 undergrads how they felt about drinking. They also asked them how they thought the average student felt about it. Participants generally said that they felt less okay with heavy drinking at college than the hypothetical average student. But it turns out that this was actually something a lot of people said. In other words, most people thought their peers were way more okay with heavy drinking than they actually were.

Recent studies have also confirmed that pluralistic ignorance plays a role in all kinds of other situations, too, from cigarette smoking and drug use to beliefs about mental health treatments. So it's not only relevant to that lecture your high school teachers might have given you before you went off to college.

The nice thing is, though, this concept can also help you resist peer pressure. See, people often give in to something because they assume everyone agrees it's right. So psychologists have suggested that, if you know about pluralistic ignorance, it might reduce the pressure you feel to conform with the group, and research has backed this up.

In a 1998 study with 143 college students, knowing about pluralistic ignorance helped one group drink less, compared to students who didn't learn about it. And a 2018 study about gender norms showed similar results. When men were shown that most people were in favor of gender equality, they were more likely to say they supported it as well, compared to groups who were told something else. While there may have been other variables at play in both of these studies, this suggests that having a little psychology knowledge in your back pocket can totally help you out in the real world. It's like having a secret window into your friends' brains.

So, the next time someone puts on that horrible playlist, speak up. You may find that other people were just as uncomfortable as you were, but didn't want to be the first person to admit it.

(Adapted from *nerdfighteria.info*)

Passage Two

Proven Strategies for Coping with Your Stress

Elizabeth Scott

When coping with stress, it can sometimes be difficult to know where to even begin, though there is no shortage of advice that may come your way. Should you tackle the problem head-on? Or should you simply change how you think about the stressors you face? Is there a specific way to make your stress dissolve so that coping with stress becomes a no-brainer? And how can you best choose the appropriate method for coping with stress?

The bad news is that it's not always easy to cope with stress. It's usually a process, and the "right answer" isn't always clear. The good news is that it becomes easier and easier to cope with stress once you become aware of what works best for you and in which situations each strategy is most helpful.

More good news is that there are few "wrong answers" when it comes to coping. It's usually a case of choosing between strategies that work "okay" and strategies that work "great", depending on your situation. (There are a few unhealthy responses to stress that you should look out for, however, like excessive drinking or obsessive worrying, but most of the coping strategies you intentionally use are helpful to some degree.)

There are several different strategies that people use for coping with stress, and each type of coping strategy brings unique benefits. Finding the best match of strategies for your situation is the key to maximizing your stress management efforts. Simply put, when coping with stress, the following two main strategies are useful: solution-based coping and appraisal-based coping.

Solution-based coping with stress

When someone employs solution-based coping strategies for coping with stress, they work to identify areas of their lives that can be changed, and follow a plan that will bring about change.

Solution-based coping includes eliminating stressors, like quitting a stressful job, breaking up with a toxic partner, or paring down a busy schedule, as a means of eliminating the stress before you encounter more of it.

This solution-based approach can be an extremely effective technique for coping with stress, and many of the uncomfortable emotions we experience along with stress such as anxiety, anger and frustration are signals that changes need to be made.

Sometimes, however, we find ourselves in stressful situations where we can't make changes in our lives and can't eliminate the stressors that we experience. For example, we might be working at a job we can't easily leave, and need to get along with difficult co-workers. We may find that our partner causes us stress, but is worth staying with anyway. We may find that every activity in our busy schedule is vital, and can't be eliminated. In cases like these, we still have the option of appraisal-based coping with stress.

Appraisal-based coping with stress

This strategy of coping with stress involves how we feel about the stressors we face throughout the day.

Appraisal-based coping strategies include cognitive restructuring, positive thinking, and humor.

Asking yourself whether something really needs to cause stress or can just be accepted as part of life, finding the humor in the ridiculousness of a stressful situation, and finding someone who seems to be coping with stress in a particular way and exploring his or her attitude are all effective appraisal-based coping strategies.

A word from *VERYWELL*

While solution-based and appraisal-based coping mechanisms can both offer relief, it's sometimes difficult to know when something can (and should) be changed versus when it should be dealt with through acceptance. In fact, the famous serenity prayer that's been so helpful in programs like AA is all about these two styles of coping: "God grant me the strength to change what I can, the patience to accept what I can't change, and the wisdom to know the difference." Often, the most effective approach is one that includes both coping strategies.

(Adapted from *verywellmind.com*)

References

Remez Sasson. Different Types of Happiness. *Success Consciousness*. Retrieved from https://www.successconsciousness.com/blog/happiness-fun/what-is-happiness/ on March 15th, 2021.

Elizabeth Scott. (2020). Different Types of Happiness. *Verywellmind*. Retrieved from https://www.verywellmind.com/happiness-types-4173234 on March 15th, 2021.

Karen Hopkin. (2017). Can Money Buy Happiness?. *Scientific American*. Retrieved from https://www.scientificamerican.com/podcast/episode/to-buy-happiness-spend-money-on-saving-time/ on March 15th, 2021.

David G. Myers. (2000). Money Can't Guarantee Happiness. *David Myers*. Retrieved from http://www.davidmyers.org/Brix? pageID=49 on March 15th, 2021.

Mckinsey Company. (2019). Read the Following News and Share Your Opinions on China Luxury. *Mckinsey*. Retrieved from https://www.mckinsey.com/~/media/McKinsey/Featured%20Insights/China/How%20young%20Chinese%20consumers%20are%20reshaping%20global%20luxury/McKinsey-China-luxury-report-2019-How-young-Chinese-consumers-are-reshaping-global-luxury.ashx on March 15th, 2021.

Gilbert Ross. (2010). Does Happiness Come from Process?. *Dumblittleman*. Retrieved from https://www.dumblittleman.com/7-life-lessons-i-learned-that-changed/ on March 15th, 2021.

Yasemin Saplakoglu. (2019). Purposeful Life Brings Happiness. *Live Science*. Retrieved from https://www.livescience.com/65552-life-purpose-mortality-decrease.html on March 15th, 2021.

Do a Country's Inhabitants Get Happier as It Gets Richer?. *The Economist*. Retrieved from https://gbr.businessreview.global/articles/view/5dadd9c094641e2c935ff3f6/en_GB/zh_CN on March 15th, 2021.

Mind Tool Content Team. What Is Stress?. *Mindtools*. Retrieved from https://www.mindtools.com/pages/article/newTCS_00.htm on March 15th, 2021.

Jerry Kennard. (2020). What Is Stress?. *Verywellmind*. Retrieved from https://www.verywellmind.com/recognizing-stress-for-men-2329008 on March 15th, 2021.

David DiSalvo. (2019). Stress Changes the Brain. *Forbes*. Retrieved from https://www.forbes.com/sites/daviddisalvo/2019/07/26/stress-changes-the-brain-and-this-could-be-how-it-happens/? sh=2f0f6ace30d5 on March 15th, 2021.

Robert Sanders. (2013). Some Stress Is Good for People. *Berkeley News*. Retrieved from https://news.berkeley.edu/2013/04/16/researchers-find-out-why-some-stress-is-good-for-you/ on March 15th, 2021.

Amy Gallo. (2011). How Can We Reduce Our Stress?. *Harvard Business Review*.

Retrieved from https://hbr.org/2011/06/turning-stress-into-an-asset on March 15th, 2021.
Brit Garner. Can We Resist Peer Pressure?. *Nerdfighteria*. Retrieved from https://www.nerdfighteria.info/v/uME3JOM3W4k/ on March 15th, 2021.
Elizabeth Scott. (2020). Proven Strategies for Coping with Your Stress. *Verywellmind*. Retrieve from https://www.verywellmind.com/tips-for-coping-with-stress-3145186 on March 15th, 2021.
Need a Rival or Not?. *Xyen*. Retrieved from https://www.xyen.com.cn/reading/2020422320/ on March 26th, 2021.
How Can Peer Pressure Affect Us?. *Research Matic*. Retrieved from https://www.researchomatic.com/peer-pressure-and-teen-pregnancy-122889.html on March 15th, 2021.
Arlin Cuncic. (2020). How to Find Happiness in Your Life?. *Verywellmind*. Retrieved from https://www.verywellmind.com/how-to-find-happiness-4584480 on March 15th, 2021.

Unit 3 Technology

Part A Technology and Human Health

A1. Introduction

Technology, Health and Health Care

Health defined in the broadest sense means a relative state in which one is able to function well physically, mentally, socially and spiritually in order to express the full range of one's unique potentialities within the environment where one is living. Currently viewed as more than the absence of disease, health is a state of optimal functioning in every aspect of one's life.

In this day and age, our health is being affected by technology almost everywhere we go. While technology adds convenience to our daily lives, these seemingly harmless devices can end up causing a lot of health concerns. Smartphones, computers and other gadgets are just some of the things that can eventually lead to bigger problems.

Being overdependent on technology can cause psychological issues such as distraction, expectation of instant gratification and even depression. Beside affecting users' mental health, use of technology can also have negative repercussions on physical health, causing vision problems, hearing loss and muscle strain. On top of that, technology is affecting the way our brain functions and develops. Specifically speaking, our attention span, decision-making, relationship building and memory capacity are all being depressed. Fortunately, there are steps that can be taken to help alleviate these health issues. Why not turn off the technology for a while, giving your mind and body the breaks they deserve?

Anyway, every single technological advance in human history has brought new economic opportunities and increased the living standards of everyone. That is because every single technological advance has leveraged the productivity of everyone. What could this mean for health care?

Technology is causing some amazing breakthroughs on the medical scene — a new, smarter age of health care. It's the path toward an entirely new system that predicts disease and delivers personalized health and wellness services to entire populations. Empowered by the vast amount of health information available online and on apps, and by the array of health and fitness wearables, many people are much less dependent on their doctors for advice.

Many health care professionals feel their jobs are at risk. Their biggest concern is that they could be replaced by machines. Yes, jobs would be lost but new ones will be created. The goal isn't to replace physicians or health care professionals, but give them better decision-making tools. Technology should integrate with the human element of the health care service and not replace it altogether. The only way to win in an artificial world is to be human. It's about incorporating new technologies but maintaining that human factor.

The debates over technology are far from being resolved, so you can take any side. It leaves space for speculation and personal evaluation. Despite great benefits from the development and use of technology, technological adoption into the medical field doesn't come without challenges. We all should be aware of the threats it may pose. After all, we are to face its intended or unintended, beneficial or harmful consequences.

(Adapted from *health. gov. au*)

A2. Passage Reading

A2. 1 Technology-induced Health Problems

The following two passages focus on the health problems that technology has induced. Read them and share your opinions according to the questions. Try to seek diverse perspectives and don't confine yourself to the reference words and expressions given.

Passage One

How Does Technology Affect Your Health?

Ann Pietrangelo

All manner of technology surrounds us. From our personal laptops, tablets and phones to **behind-the-scenes** technology that furthers medicine, science, and education. Technology is here to stay, but it's always **morphing and expanding**. As each new technology enters the scene, it has the potential to improve lives. But, in some cases, it also has the potential to negatively affect physical and emotional health. Read on as we take a look at a few possible negative effects of technology and provide tips on healthier ways to use it.

Digital eye strain

Prolonged use of computers, tablets, and cellphones can lead to digital eye strain. Symptoms may include:

- blurred vision
- dry eyes
- headaches
- neck and shoulder pain

Contributing factors are screen glare, bad lighting, and improper viewing distance. The 20-20-20 rule is recommended to ease eye strain. To follow this rule, try to take a 20-second break every 20 minutes to look at something that's 20 feet away.

Musculoskeletal problems

When you use a smartphone, the chances are that you're holding your head in an unnatural forward-leaning position. This position puts a lot of stress on your neck, shoulders and spine.

A 2017 study found a clear association between **self-reported** addiction to smartphone use and neck problems. An earlier study found that among teens, neck-shoulder pain and low back pain rose during the 1990s at the same time when the use of information and communication technology was increasing. Overuse of technology can also lead to repetitive strain injuries of the fingers, thumbs and wrists.

If you're feeling the pain of technology, you can take the following steps to reduce these issues:

- take frequent breaks to stretch
- create an **ergonomic** workspace
- maintain proper posture while using your devices

Sleep problems

Technology in the bedroom can interfere with sleep in a number of ways. According to the National Sleep Foundation, 90 percent of people in the United States say that they use tech devices in the hour before going to bed, which can be physiologically and psychologically stimulating enough to affect sleep.

The exposure to the blue light that devices emit can **suppress melatonin** and **interrupt your circadian clock**. Both of these effects can make it harder to fall asleep and result in you being less alert in the morning. Having electronic devices in the bedroom places temptation **at your fingertips**, and it can make **switching off** more difficult. That, in turn, can make it harder to **drift off** when you try to sleep.

Emotional problems

Using social media can make you feel more connected to the world. But, comparing yourself to others can leave you **feeling inadequate** or left out. A recent study looked at the social media use of more than 1,700 people between the ages of 19 and 32. The researchers found that those with high social media use **felt more socially isolated** than those who spent less time on social media. They also noted that there might be an association between **problematic Internet use** and **depression**, **substance use** and **aggressive behavior.**

However, the researchers noted that whether it has a beneficial or **detrimental effect** depends on the quality of social factors in the social network environment. More research is necessary to make conclusions on **cause and effect.** If social media use makes you feel anxious or depressed, try cutting back to see if doing so makes a difference.

Positive effects of technology

Technology plays a role in virtually every part of our lives, whether we're aware of it or not. These are just a few of the ways in which technology may positively affect our physical and mental health:

- health apps to **track chronic illnesses** and communicate vital information to doctors
- health apps that help you **track diet**, exercise, and mental health information
- online medical records that give you access to test results and allow you to **fill prescriptions**
- **virtual doctor visits**
- online education and ease of research
- enhanced communication with others, which can improve the feeling of connection

Ways to make the most of technology

With each new advance in technology, it gets a bit easier to **go overboard.** When we get too caught up in it, we can feel it in our minds and bodies. So, how much is too much?

The answer is as individual as you are. Here are some signs that you might be **leaning too heavily on technology**:

- Your family or friends complain about your tech use.
- You've neglected relationships in favor of technology, which people sometimes refer to as **phubbing.**
- It has interfered with your work.
- You're losing sleep or **skipping physical activities** due to technology use.
- It's causing you stress or anxiety, or you're noticing **physical side effects**, such as

tension headaches, eye strain, muscle pain or overuse injuries.

- You can't seem to stop.

If that sounds familiar, here are some ways to **cut back on screen time**:

- Clear your phone of unessential apps to keep you from constantly **checking it for updates.**
- **Carve out** a specific, limited amount of time to use your devices.
- Keep electronic devices out of the bedroom. Charge them in another room.
- Make mealtime **gadget-free time.**
- **Prioritize** real-world relationships over online relationships.

Closing words

Technology is a part of our lives. It can have some negative effects, but it can also offer many positive benefits and play an important role in education, health, and general welfare. Knowing the possible negative effects can help you take steps to identify and minimize them so that you can still enjoy the positive aspects of technology.

(Adapted from *healthline. com*)

☞**Notes**

- **ergonomic**: It is relating to the design of furniture or equipment which makes it comfortable and effective for people who use it.
- **melatonin**: It is a hormone in the body that produces changes in skin color and is involved in controlling biorhythms such as our sleep pattern.
- **circadian clock**: It is an internal biological clock we each have that organizes the internal and external activities of our body around the 24-hour day.
- **go overboard**: It means to do something too much, or to be too excited or eager about something.
- **phubbing**: It refers to the act of ignoring someone you are with and giving attention to your mobile phone instead.

Passage Two

How Is Modern Technology Affecting Human Brains?

Walden University

The Internet and digital technology may be impacting our physical and psychological development to a larger degree than we expected. In the last few decades, technology has progressed **at a staggering rate.** Smartphones, the Internet, **cloud computing** and hundreds of other inventions are changing **every facet of our lives.** Communication, business, government, travel, **fundraising** and even agriculture have been affected. But how about our brains? Is all this new technology changing us on the inside? Many think so, including psychology professionals.

As *Psychology Today* says, "There is little doubt that all of the new technologies, led by the Internet and digital technology, are shaping the way we think in ways obvious and subtle, deliberate and unintentional, and advantageous and detrimental." While research into this field is still **in its infancy** and there are no scientifically **agreed-upon conclusions**, there are several areas where modern digital technology is certainly affecting the way we interact with the world and the way our children's brains develop. These areas include:

Attention

Evidence suggests that short **attention spans** are one of the results of the continuous use of mobile technology and the Internet. Our average attention span has decreased by 4 seconds, down from 12 to 8, which is shorter than that of a goldfish. Significant increase in distractions created by **digital notifications and reminders** is one of the main reasons for reduced attention spans.

When we all have computers or smartphones in our pockets that allow us to play games, listen to music, and connect with friends whenever we want, why should we **tolerate boredom**? Of course, this shortened attention span likely **comes with consequences**. How many times do we miss important conversations or moments happening around us because we're **mesmerized** by our electronic devices?

Decision-making

You need to buy a new car. What's the first thing you do? If you're like millions of others, you go online to do research. In this modern world, we are more likely to turn to our Internet-connected mobile devices when it comes to making a decision. Whether we want to find out the best restaurant in the town for dinner or select a profitable career path, Google is our best companion that helps us make the right decisions.

It shows that we as humans, no longer have to depend on **emotional instinct**. Instead, we go to the web and collect more information, details and facts with an intention to make wise decisions. The latest technology provides us with **ample information**, data and facts that can be used to **make informed decisions**, in every walk of life.

Relationship building

Social media has connected almost 50% of the entire global population. It helps people **raise their voices** and make their voices heard by billions of people using social media platforms. We can also interact with friends, family members and business-related people across the globe even in real-time. We're **radically** changing the way we can build and maintain relationships.

But is this a good or bad thing? If we're at dinner with friends and are **simultaneously** texting a family member in California and **tweeting with** acquaintances about an event in Japan, are we **fully engaged in** any of those relationships? Then again, doesn't being able to stay connected with friends and family around the world keep relationships alive that might otherwise **wither**? Nearly 70% of Americans think the Internet is good for our relationships, but it remains to be seen if children who are growing up with smartphones develop the kinds of **interpersonal and relationship-building skills** they need to form deep and meaningful relationships, or if our species will become isolated from — and uncomfortable with — close, personal contact.

Memory

The Internet gives us access to a huge amount of information; plus, our personal computers can store every shopping list and **stray thought** we have, letting us access the information when we need it later. A new study finds that this **pervasive access to information** has not only changed what we remember; it has also changed how we remember. Our reliance on the Internet has decreased our ability to easily **retain facts.** However, we appear to be improving our ability to remember where and how to **locate information.** For instance, we are now more likely to remember what **folder** we stored information in than we are to remember the information itself. Likewise, we remember the keywords and **search terms** that can help us find the solutions and **uncover answers** instead of remembering the facts that are useful even if there is no Internet connection.

Takeaway

Technology is out there to help us in many ways. It helps us learn effectively, communicate faster and get smarter in ways we do things. At the same time, it could also be a bad thing for us to waste time on useless activities and **numb ourselves to** all the emotions we should take good care of. That's why we should use mobile technology and other gadgets properly and wisely, to prevent side effects coming with it.

(Adapted from *waldenu. edu*)

☞**Notes**

- **mesmerize**: It means to have one's attention completely so that one cannot think of anything else.
- **tweeting with**: It is communicating with somebody on Twitter using quick short messages.
- **stray thoughts**: They are thoughts or ideas that occur to you by chance.
- **takeaway**: It refers to a main message or piece of information that you learn from something you hear or read.

Opinion sharing

(a) Does technology make your life healthier? Give reasons.
(b) Is the Internet depressing your learning ability? Why?
(c) Does technology make you a better decision maker? Give reasons.
(d) Is social media making you more connected or more isolated? Why?
(e) Should we designate tech-free times for college students? Give reasons.
(f) Re-evaluate how you feel with and without digital devices.

Reference Words and Expressions

overuse	过度使用
overburden	使不堪重负
sleep-deprived	缺乏睡眠的
overdependent	过度依赖的
disconnected	分离的，不关联的
attention-deficit	注意力缺乏的
distracted	注意力分散的
depression	抑郁(症)
multitasker	同时应对多个任务的人
unplug	拔下(电器的电源插头)

heavy users of the Internet	互联网的重度使用者
tech-obsessed world	痴迷于技术的世界
cutting-edge technology	领先技术
well-researched phenomenon	被深入调查的现象
handheld device	手持设备
incorrect / awkward posture	错误/别扭的姿势
reduce physical strain	减少身体负担/拉伤
ward off adverse effect	避开不利影响
sedentary behavior	久坐行为
skip physical exercise	逃避锻炼
increased risk of obesity	患肥胖症风险增加
muscle and joint injury	肌肉和关节损伤
premature death	过早死亡
failing memory	下降的记忆力
independent thinker	独立思考者
social incompatibility	不合群(指社交方面)
emotional instability	情绪不稳定

fear of missing out	害怕错过
filter out irrelevant information	过滤掉不相关信息
handle the barrage of information	处理接二连三的信息
switch tasks	转换/切换任务
social media platform	社交媒体平台
digital native	数字原住民
holiday snaps	度假照片
snap photos	迅速大量拍照
post... on the Moments	发朋友圈
hide one's post	隐藏某人发布的信息
add... as my WeChat friend	加……为微信好友
image editing software	形象编辑软件
fix one's flaw	弥补自己的缺陷
crop / resize / blur a picture	剪裁/调整尺寸/模糊处理照片
blurry picture	模糊的照片
take real-to-life selfies	真实自拍
make approving / nasty comments	好评/恶评
turn off / refresh notifications	关闭/刷新通知
be obsessed with likes and comments	痴迷于点赞和评论
click the like button / give a like	点赞
thumbs up / down	赞成/反对
take a screenshot / screen-cap	截屏
side-text somebody	与某人私聊
somebody is blacklisted / blocked	某人被拉黑/屏蔽
unfollow / unfriend	取消关注/删除好友
curb Internet addiction	控制网瘾
provide interesting alternatives	提供(其他)有趣的选择
cut back on screen time	减少屏幕时间

Speaking Activities

Individual talk

It's not hard to find examples of how technology is negatively affecting young people, the most digitally connected population in history. Their constant connection to various modern gadgets may cause both short-term and long-term health problems. Should we lay all the blame at the feet of technology?

Discussion

"Screen time" is a term used for activities done in front of a screen, such as watching TV, working on a computer, using a cell phone or playing video games. Screen time is sedentary activity, meaning you are being physically inactive while sitting down.

(a) How much is your average screen time per day?
(b) What takes up most of your screen time?
(c) How is your health being affected as a result?
(d) How to cut back on your screen time?

Debate

Multitasking

At any given moment you might be texting a friend, switching between multiple windows on your computer, listening to the blare of the television and talking on the phone all at once! Modern tech has made multitasking the norm in our life. We always perform a number of tasks simultaneously and rapidly, switching back and forth from one thing to another.

(Adapted from *verywellmind.com*)

Topic for debate: Multitaskers are losing the ability to focus.

A2.2 Technology-affected Health Care

The following two passages focus on the health care that has been affected by technology. Read them and share your opinions according to the questions. Try to seek diverse perspectives and don't confine yourself to the reference words and expressions given.

Passage One

Is Technology the Health Care Wave of the Future?

Elaine Cox

In today's world, we are driven by instant access to whatever we want. After all, you can do everything via an app: **set up rides**, pay bills, order food for delivery and shop for anything that can often be delivered overnight. Convenience has become the most important commodity.

This information and convenience revolution has had a significant positive impact on society. We can **ease the tensions** of our day, from booking a flight to ordering dinner, which means we save time and energy for other work and leisure activities. And we can connect with people across the world for business or friendship. Connections abound!

However, when it comes to technology and health care, it does pose certain questions — opportunities and challenges, often both contained in the same scenario.

Let's start with access to care. **Telemedicine** can allow care and access to specialists across long distances. Often, people can be virtually seen by a provider — and get both a diagnosis and **prescribed treatment** — without leaving their home. One may wonder how long before we'll be **"streaming"** all but the most complex health care interactions.

In addition, there are many **patient portals.** These allow for all kinds of interactions regarding our health needs without ever involving the team. **Scheduling appointments, refilling prescriptions** and even **viewing lab results** are readily accomplished via technology. It gives people access to their records and fulfills their needs without leaving their couch.

In the world today, those options may seem to be absolutely on point. We would expect all those metrics we measure to improve — access, flow and satisfaction. A whole new era of medical care could be **on the horizon.** But of course, as we're taught in 6th grade science class, for every action there is an equal and opposite reaction. And what those reactions might be **in a new techno-health care era** needs to be explored.

First of all, we should think about the entire health care experience on a continuum and not just **siloed** in one acute episode. Take the usual interaction with a doctor. The visit begins with office staff, which can be very insightful into how someone is doing. Take, for example, the elderly patient who's having trouble remembering things. This may impact **medication compliance** and other aspects of general **health hygiene.** Or the young mother who may be struggling with **post-partum depression.** The front lines at the door often note these subtle clues that something is going on. It's unlikely that a portal or streaming service will have such intuition.

Next, the actual **medical encounter.** The **bond** between a patient and his or her provider has been **sacrosanct** for **eons.** The whole reason for the design of the medical home is to have a history that can be used for context on the health care journey. Sharing the intimate details of one's life in any relationship requires trust, which takes time to build. This is definitely true in health care, where some of life's best and worst moments involve one's doctor. The human touch should not be underestimated and is unlikely to occur via a smartphone or streaming box.

Lastly, **test results** can be — at best — difficult to interpret, and at worst, lead to devastating news. In the past, doctors would review these results and call and offer more than just a number or formal reading. They would **interpret the results** into something meaningful, and hopefully the delivery was **with compassion.** When someone who doesn't have a medical degree opens a portal and sees a **flagged, abnormal result** with no interpretation, there's room for all kinds of stories to form in their minds — plus great anxiety that may not even be necessary, as not every flagged result is clinically significant depending on the patient complaint. However, the workload of the physician can often result in delays hearing back on much anticipated results. Sometimes that means **late-day phone calls**, after office hours and when no one has much energy to talk.

So how does medicine adapt to the new technology age? How do we find a space where patients can be satisfied with their access and the transparency of the system? How can we create a space where doctors can be **expedient** with their time management but still retain the therapeutic relationship and provide much needed context for their patients? How can we stay true to our mission as a health care system to guide our patients through whatever journey they're experiencing, if we rarely engage outside a computer program?

Very talented companies are working on this dilemma. There are even sources for medical equipment that can be used by a patient at home to transmit vital signs and heart sounds through telemedicine. Some physicians and other providers are now routinely **offering telemedicine visits** to maintain continuity with their patients. It seems likely that some artificial intelligence company will come up with a way to give context to test results. It will all be accurate and expedient.

But what it will not achieve is the warmth of human interaction and touch. Patients often need someone to listen to — and care about — their journey story. Physicians need **validation** that their reason for going to medical school, which was most assured that they wanted to help people, is still true. These attributes will never be realized through **a sterile, human-less technology**. It should be a tool, but using it as a total solution will most definitely have consequences that were unanticipated. Let's not allow our **humanity** to be one of them — whether we're giving or receiving.

(Adapted from *health. usnews. com*)

☞**Notes**

- **portal**: It is a page on the Internet that allows people to get useful information, such as news and weather, and to find other websites.
- **siloed**: It means to be separated from other people or things.
- **sacrosanct**: It is so important that there cannot be any change or question.
- **eon**: It refers to a period of time that is so long that it cannot be measured.
- **expedient**: It is helpful or useful in a particular situation, but sometimes not morally acceptable.

Passage Two

AI Can't Replace Doctors but Make Them Better

Rahul Parikh

Several years ago, a Silicon Valley investor, wrote a provocative article titled "Do We Need Doctors or Algorithms?". He argued that doctors were no match for artificial intelligence. Doctors **banter with** patients, gather a few symptoms, hunt around the body for clues, and send the patient off with a prescription. This sometimes (accidentally, maybe) leads to the correct treatment, but doctors are acting on only a fraction of the available information. An **algorithm**, he wrote, could do better.

I'm a **pediatric and adolescent physician** in the San Francisco Bay Area, where entrepreneurs like that Silicon Valley investor have been knocking on the doors of doctors for years with their **pilot technologies** and software and hardware. I can say with some authority that these entrepreneurs are the voice of **a savvy outsider** who knows what he knows — which isn't health care.

Yes, AI could help us diagnose and treat disease. It can **collate** and **serve up** broad **swaths of data** in a clear and concise way, cutting down on the imprecise judgments that doctors make because of the pressures and complexity of our practices. There's no doubt that for certain doctors, whose work is highly focused on diagnosis (radiologists or pathologists, for example), that breakthrough may **prove an existential threat.** A decade ago, for example, researchers showed that AI was as good as radiologists at **detecting breast cancer.**

But for physicians like me in primary care, managing 1,500 to 2,000 patients, AI presents an opportunity. I went to medical school to connect with people and make a difference. Today I often feel like an overpaid bookkeeper instead, **taking in information** and **spitting it back** to patients, **prescribing drugs** and **adjusting doses**, **ordering tests.** But AI in the exam room opens up the chance to recapture the art of medicine. It could let me get to know my patients better, learn how a disease uniquely affects them, and give me time to coach them toward a better outcome.

Consider what AI could do for asthma, the most common chronic medical disease in childhood. Six million American kids suffer from it. In 2013, they collectively missed 14 million days of school. The cost of medications, visits to the doctor and emergency room, and hospitalizations nears $60 billion a year.

I diagnose asthma via **a rule of thumb** that's been handed down over time: if you've had three or more wheezing episodes and the medicines for asthma help, you have the disease. Once it's diagnosed, I ask the parents to remember — as best they can — how often they **administer medicines to their child.** I ask: What seems to trigger episodes? Is the child exposed to anyone who smokes at home? I can also review their records to count how many visits to the emergency room they've had, or the number of times they've refilled their prescriptions. But even with the most accurate recall by parents and patients, and the most accurate electronic records, it's still just **retrospective knowledge.** There's no proactive, predictive strategy.

It's not that we don't have the data; it's just that it's messy. **Reams of data clog** the physician's in-box. It comes in many forms and from disparate directions: objective information such as lab results and vital signs, subjective concerns that come in the form of phone messages or e-mails from patients. It's all fragmented, and we spend a great deal of our time as physicians trying to make sense of it. Technology companies and **fledging startups** want to open the **data spigot** even further by letting their direct-to-consumer devices — phone, watch, **blood-pressure cuff**, **blood-sugar meter** — send continuous streams of numbers directly to us. We struggle to keep up with it, and the rates of **burnout** among doctors continue to rise.

How can AI fix this? Let's start with diagnosis. While the clinical manifestations of asthma are easy to spot, the disease is much more complex **at a molecular and cellular level.** The genes, proteins, enzymes, and other drivers of asthma are highly diverse, even if their **environmental triggers overlap.** Ian Adock of the National Heart & Lung Institute at Imperial College, London, studies the link between asthma and the environment. He and his team have been collecting biological samples from asthma patients' blood, urine and lung tissue and organizing the genetic and molecular markers he finds into subtypes of asthma. The hypothesis is that with that kind of knowledge, patients can be given the drug that works best for them.

AI might also help to manage asthma flares. For many patients, asthma gets worse as air pollution levels rise. AI could let us take environmental information and respond proactively. In 2015, researchers published a study showing they could predict the number of asthma-related emergency room visits to a Dallas-Fort Worth hospital. They **pulled data from** patient records, along with air pollution data from EPA sensors.

If I had this kind of data I could say, "Alexa, tell me which asthma patients I need to worry about today." I could **give a heads-up** to the affected families. And if I also had some genetic data, I could diagnose asthma before the patient suffered three **bouts** of wheezing, by ordering blood tests and comparing the results against those molecular markers.

This kind of time-saving intelligence frees me to spend more time with my patients and allows me more time to personally interact with those kids, and get better results.

Lots of questions lie ahead. Are patients willing to share more of their personal data with us? If the AI shows your care is better one way, but you or your doctor feel differently, will an insurance company accept it? What if the algorithm misses something or is applied incorrectly? Who is liable, the doctor or the machine's maker? Not long ago, in the *Journal of the American Medical Association*, I saw a colorful picture drawn by a child in crayon. It portrayed her pediatrician, eyes **glued to** the computer, while she sat on the exam table, looking **wide-eyed**. I hope that AI will soon allow me to turn my attention back to that little girl.

(Adapted from *technologyreview.com*)

> ☞ **Notes**
> - **give a heads-up**: It means to tell somebody that something is going to happen.
> - **bout**: It is a short period of illness or involvement in an activity.

Opinion sharing

(a) How has technology helped you monitor and improve your health at home?
(b) How has technology transformed the way you approach medical treatment?
(c) When would you prefer a virtual doctor visit to an in-person one?
(d) What kinds of patients might be marginalized by telemedicine? Why?
(e) What is your view on the phenomenon that traditional Chinese medicine, which is much less reliant on technology, is gaining more popularity abroad?

Reference Words and Expressions

telehealth / telemedicine	远程就医
revolutionize	变革
cost-effective	划算的，有成本效益的
misinformation	错误信息
misdiagnosis	误诊
disparity	差异，不平等
tech-savvy	懂技术的
time-pressed	时间紧迫的
fast-tracking	快速跟进的
pandemic	流行病；流行的
health care provider / health professional	医疗保健工作者
a virtual doctor visit	虚拟问诊
an integral part of...	是……不可或缺的一部分
hard-to-reach community	难以到达的社区

beyond geographic border	超越地理边界
e-consultation / in-person consultation	电子咨询/当面咨询
free up precious beds in hospitals	空出宝贵的医院床位
shelter-in-place order	原地避难/留在原地
at-risk individual	可能受到影响的个体,疑似个体
track-and-trace app	追踪应用程序
launch contactless delivery service	启动非接触式送货服务
under home quarantine	居家隔离
social distancing	社交距离
wearable fitness device	可穿戴的健康装置
personalized health-management tool	个性化的健康管理工具
electronic medical record	电子病历
gather big data in minimal time	在最少时间内收集大量数据
continual feedback	持续的反馈
public health emergencies	突发公共卫生事件
clinician shortage	临床医生短缺
juggle busy schedule	应对繁忙的日程
suffer burnout	感到疲劳过度
time stress	时间压力
schedule an appointment	预约见面
cancel non-urgent appointment	取消非紧急预约
clinical face time with patient	门诊时间
fill a prescription	开处方
over-the-counter medication	非处方药
administer medications to sb.	给某人用药
prescribe medications to sb.	给某人开药
drug dosing recommendation	药物使用剂量(一般由医生建议)
imaging test	影像检测
take a CT scan	做电脑断层扫描
take an X-ray	做 X 光检查
technology-driven diagnosis	技术驱动的诊断
erode diagnostic skill	逐步破坏诊断技能
rates of hospitalization	住院率
a rule of thumb	经验法则
hands-on experience	实践经验
in the foreseeable future	在可预见的未来
robotic surgery / robot-assisted surgery	机器人手术
traditional open surgery	传统开放式手术

minimally invasive 微创的
innate humanness 先天的人性
crave human interaction 渴望人际互动

Speaking Activities

Individual talk

Surgical Robots

According to a study, a total of 144 deaths, 1,391 patient injuries and 8,061 device malfunctions were reported with robotic surgery during a 14-year period. The most common robotic-surgery malfunctions include error code bugs, imaging problems, burnt or broken pieces of instruments and unintended operation of instruments. Once a malfunction occurs, surgeons have to wait for the system to restart, or switch to non-robotic techniques and reschedule procedures.

(Adapted from *mcgowanhood. com*)

Would you choose a robotic surgery if there was an alternative to it? Give your reasons.

Discussion

During the COVID-19 pandemic, technologies are playing a crucial role in keeping our society functional in a time of lockdowns and quarantines. And these technologies may have a long-lasting impact beyond the COVID-19 pandemic.

(a) How does technology help reduce the spread of the coronavirus?
(b) What industries have stayed open with the help of technology during the pandemic?
(c) How did technology make your home quarantine easier during the pandemic?

Debate

Nurses Are Here to Stay

You can create a machine to do tasks, but it's very difficult to get one to look at a patient holistically and make assessments and judgment calls. That's where nurses will always have the "advantage". You can enter symptoms into a computer and have it spit something out, but that still doesn't mean it's an accurate assessment, and it just simply cannot take everything into consideration. Nurses offer a lot of things that machines cannot.

(Adapted from *allnurses. com*)

Topic for debate: Nurses will never lose their jobs to machines.

A3. Extensive Reading

Is GPS Dangerous to Your Health?

George Michelsen Foy

We are addicted to GPS, and this addiction puts us in danger.

I can hear the protests already: What do you mean? I use it all the time, it's great, I can drive the kids to their sleepover in a neighborhood I've never been in before without worry or delay! Where's the problem?

Bear with me.

It's true, addiction to a global positioning satellite system (GPS) isn't as melodramatic or tragic as alcoholism or opioid addiction.

And it's a fact that GPS is a hugely accurate and important tool. The computer systems that run our financial, communications and power grids are mostly keyed to GPS time signals. The trucks, ships and aircraft that make commerce possible rely on GPS direction. These satellite systems even guide combine harvesters as they slash their way back and forth across Iowa cornfields.

But look what happens when we blindly follow GPS directions. In a suburb of Boston, a woman obeying her GPS drives her car onto the commuter railroad tracks, and barely manages to haul her kids out before the Fitchburg local smashes the car to scrap metal. In Alaska, a driver, also mindlessly obeying a device, steers his car off a dock, straight into Prince William Sound. In California, a child dies in Death Valley because of a GPS mistake.

Across the world, a native Londoner hands the cabbie her smartphone, on which is displayed the address to which she wants to go. The cab driver asks, "Do you know this area, love?" She replies no, she has no need to learn her city, the GPS does it for her. The driver, who has memorized every one of London's 23,000 streets and byways to earn his license, is shocked.

It's not just a person-by-person problem. GPS-based systems, which rely on signals from 39 satellites flying in extremely high orbit, 20,000 kilometers above the planet's surface, are vulnerable because of their signal's relative weakness. In 2009 the Federal Aviation Administration's Newark, NJ, air traffic control system, newly converted to satellite tracking, shut down when its GPS feed went dead. This happened every day at roughly the same time. The culprit was eventually located: it was a truck driver, daily cruising the same route near the airport, who had installed an off-the-shelf GPS jammer so his boss, who was monitoring his position, wouldn't know where he was or when he was taking a leisurely lunch break. A similar incident shut down Newark in 2013.

Even the U. S. Navy, possibly the most technologically advanced force in world history, is taking notice. A decade after removing them from the curriculum, the U. S. Navy Academy recently reinstated courses in celestial navigation for fear that wartime impairment or destruction of global positioning networks would leave Navy commanders, and their ships, aircraft and weapons systems, lost and defenseless.

According to a hacker who works for a European secret service, professional hackers working for a hostile country could shut down most of America's power grid in five minutes by corrupting or jamming the GPS time link that coordinates electrical supply networks.

More personal perils exist.

Robotic reliance on GPS-type electronic aids, and associated disuse of the navigational centers in our brain, increase our likelihood of contracting neurological diseases like Alzheimer's and dementia, according to researchers at McGill, University College London and Washington University.

Another, subtler, but possibly just as serious danger stems from such addiction.

Humans evolved and progressed by seeking to explore and understand the unknown. Anthropologists believe the descendants of a few hundred hunter-gatherers, starting in south-central Africa, discovered and populated every corner of the planet except Antarctica in less than 50,000 years. Homo sapiens' consciousness, wrapped around the hippocampal formation — a neutral structure that navigates space, memory, and associated emotions — was perfected in the process.

Exploring the unknown as our ancestors did means, very exactly, not knowing where we are to start with, physically, intellectually or both. It means getting lost.

So what will happen to the hippocampal formation, this amazing organ that navigates not only the world but our memory of the world, our recall of everything, and thus our very identity, when we stop navigating on our own because a machine now does all the navigating for us?

To rely constantly on a GPS-enabled smartphone, which tells us where we are geographically every second of the day, pulls us out of the habit of thinking in the oldest, most human way there is: I'm lost, where should I go now, how do I find my way? It's not surprising that atrophy and disease result from this sort of intellectual surrender.

(Adapted from *thedailybeast.com*)

Part B Technology and Ethical Dilemmas

B1. Introduction

Technology Causes Ethical Dilemmas

Individuals and organizations use technology to enhance their daily operations, be it business, learning, construction or therapeutic activities. Though many positive outcomes have arisen from modern technologies, social and ethical problems have proven to be the major obstacles and hindrances to their development. With the new power of accessible cyber communication, rapid automation of many routine tasks and the new perspective of exploration for information held within the world, issues have arisen in the topics ranging from social inequality and responsibility to personal privacy and security, thus increasing awareness of the impact of technology on society and its coming generations.

These issues all should make us stop and think — at what point do the negatives of innovation overshadow the good that it may bring? And is there ever an innovation so beneficial to the world that it would be worth compromising on ethics in order to achieve scientific and technological progress?

Advancement in technology does not elicit ethical issues, but it is the use of technological inventions that raises these issues and creates ethical dilemmas. Ultimately, how we approach the regulation of emerging technologies will inevitably have wide implications — not only for security and ethics, but for our definition of human dignity and equality of individuals.

(Adapted from *forbes.com*)

B2. Passage Reading

B2.1 Equality and Morality

The following two passages focus on the ethical dilemmas that technology creates in social equality and responsibilities. Read them and share your opinions according to the questions. Try to seek diverse perspectives and don't confine yourself to the reference words and expressions given.

Passage One

Can Technology Offer Solutions to Inequality?

Kentaro Toyama

America is seeing levels of inequality it hasn't experienced for a century. And if you believe some **technologists**, that can be addressed with **gadgets.** For example, here's Facebook CEO **Mark Zuckerberg** talking about the Internet: "The richest 500 million (people in the world) have **way more** money than the next six billion combined. You solve that by getting everyone online."

This view isn't limited to Silicon Valley. "Technology is a **game-changer** in the field of education," says U. S. Secretary of Education. It will "improve achievement for all and increase equity for children." In 2011, **then-Secretary of State** Hillary Clinton announced a new foreign policy doctrine called "Internet freedom". She said that information networks could **alleviate global poverty** because they are **"a great leveler".**

But does technology really address inequality?

Over the last decade, I've looked hard for ways in which digital devices can help the world's poorest communities. Together with colleagues in India, I developed text-free software to aid **non-literate** home servants in urban India. In rural Uganda, I explored electronic tools that delivered agricultural information to rural farmers. In Brazil, I studied educational technologies in government schools. In all, I've been involved in more than 50 such projects to boost agriculture, education, governance, health care, and micro finance with personal computers, mobile phones, digital cameras and other devices.

But one pattern was repeated: What people got out of technology depended on what wealth, education and **social ties** they already had. Technology is powerful, but its power depends on its human users.

This is true as much in America as elsewhere. Massively open online courses, or **MOOCs**, were once thought to bring education to **the disenfranchised.** With content made available free online, anyone with Internet access could learn, or so it was hoped. Studies show, however, that those who complete MOOCs are mostly **college-educated working professionals**, not **jobless high-school dropouts.**

Over the last four decades, America has enjoyed a golden age of digital innovation. Yet during the same span of time, the **poverty rate increased**, **social mobility stagnated** and **inequality skyrocketed.** Contrary to Zuckerberg, "getting everyone online" didn't prevent the 1% from **pulling away.**

How can it be that something that benefits so many of us could **worsen inequality**? The simple answer is that technology helps us **in proportion to** what we already have. That is to say, digital tools benefit **the haves** more than **the have-nots**; they don't add the same, fixed benefit for everyone.

This idea seems obvious, but it runs counter to the **Utopian** claims of tech **enthusiasts.** And, it has unexpected consequences: Among other things, technology widely disseminated only **amplifies inequalities. Ivy League** graduates are better equipped to learn from online courses than people who struggled through high school. Celebrities see their **social media posts** travel farther than those with a limited circle of followers. Power brokers with **a high-society Rolodex** can do more with email than a homeless person in the **inner city.** Even when the technology is the same, the outcomes **diverge.**

Technology is less a bridge, and more a jack — it **widens socio-economic gaps.**

Social entrepreneurs suggest that by offering products free or at low cost, they are **closing the digital divide** and **democratizing access.** There's no doubt that more people are on the Internet because it's free to users. But the lesson of technology's amplifying power is that democratization isn't enough. Nothing short of a deliberate **allocation of resources** in favor of the less wealthy and the less powerful can **shrink social divides** — and that decision lies with politics, not technology.

Cheaper gadgets don't change the fact that rich, powerful people can always afford more. Smart tools don't overcome the advantage of the better-educated. Even when free, technologies don't **dispel** relative advantages.

If inequality is the problem, we need something other than technological solutions.

(Adapted from *usatoday.com*)

☞**Notes**

- **disenfranchised**: It means not having the right to vote, or a similar right, or having had that right taken away.
- **Mark Zuckerberg**: He is the co-founder and CEO of the social-networking website Facebook, as well as one of the world's youngest billionaires.
- **MOOCs**: It refers to Massive Open Online Courses facilitated wholly online and designed to support an unlimited number of enrolments for free.
- **utopian**: It is relating to or aiming for a perfect society in which everyone works well with each other and is happy.
- **Ivy League**: It refers to eight respected colleges and universities in the northeast of the U. S., including Yale University, Harvard University, University of Pennsylvania, Brown University, Princeton University, Columbia University, Dartmouth College and Cornell University.
- **Rolodex**: It is a brand name for a circular file of cards on which you keep people's names and addresses.

Passage Two

AIs Continue to Act in Unpredictable Ways, Should We Panic?

John Loeffler

Researchers claim that their artificial intelligence agent has deliberately hidden data from them in order to perform a required task in a way that appears on its face to be cheating. This development has added to a growing body of evidence that the fears over an unpredictable artificial intelligence may be **well-founded.** As AIs continue to perform tasks **in novel ways** that humans simply never anticipate, how do we protect ourselves from the consequences of what we often cannot see coming?

Who's afraid of artificial intelligence... and who's not?

Easily the most visible advocate for caution when dealing with **a potential existential threat to** humanity is **Elon Musk.** The PayPal co-founder and **erstwhile** head of Tesla, **SpaceX** and the Boring Company, Musk has long been an opponent of **unregulated** AI research. He once said, "I am really quite close, I am very close, to the **cutting edge** in AI and it **scares the hell out of me.**"

He isn't alone. None other than the late **Stephen Hawking** warned about the threat to our species that artificial intelligence poses. "It would take off on its own," he said, "and re-design itself at an ever-increasing rate. Humans, who are limited by slow **biological evolution**, couldn't compete, and would be **superseded.**" He warned to humanity, "The development of full artificial intelligence could **spell the end of the human race.**"

Others find these anxieties to be **overblown**. Mark Zuckerberg said **in response to** Elon Musk's public comments on the subject of AI, "I think people who are naysayers and try to **drum up** these **doomsday scenarios** — I just don't understand it. It's really negative and in some ways, I actually think it is pretty irresponsible." He went on to add that "in the next five to ten years, AI is going to deliver so many improvements in the quality of our lives."

Everywhere you go to discuss the development of artificial intelligence, you will find this debate with very few people arguing **from a middle ground position** and both sides have some **heavyweight voices** in their camp. But which one has the weight of evidence on its side?

The good, the bad, and the singularity

Facebook and Google occupy an interesting position in that both companies are **at the forefront of** AI development, so they have produced considerable research on the subject of artificial intelligence.

In fact, it was Google researchers who found that their AI agent cheated when asked to convert a satellite photo to a map and then back again to a photo. Google needed the AI to **generate** an original map from the image and then try to recreate the image from the map it created — like translating a sentence into a foreign language and then back into the original language, without the benefit of knowing what the original statement was.

Instead, what they found was that details from the original image that were eliminated in the street map reappeared when the agent was instructed to recreate the original image. It turns out the AI saved the data it knew it would need to recreate the photo and **encoded** this data into the street map in a way that the researchers couldn't see it if they didn't know it was there.

Given a task to perform, the AI — utilizing machine learning via a neural network — found the most efficient way to complete the task by not actually performing the task at all, only pretending to. Essentially, the AI cheated because the researchers didn't explicitly forbid the AI from doing this.

The unforeseeable complexities in AI decision-making

There are many more examples of this kind of unpredicted behavior in AIs. Self-driving cars make the roads safer, without question, but sometimes they also drive through six red lights in San Francisco.

AIs can be utilized to perform all sorts of data processing tasks that will save millions of

staff-hours every year at a savings of billions of dollars, or they can decide that an empty set is a perfectly processed set, and therefore delete all of the records you ask it to handle.

In 2012, a Wall Street Hedge Fund lost control of its AI-driven trading algorithm and started **racking up** $10 million in losses every minute. It took 45-minutes for a team of programmers to find the source of the problem and stop it, minutes before the firm would have become **insolvent**.

Can we protect ourselves from unpredictable AIs?

Given the level of investment in AI technology and the benefits of harnessing AIs in every field from military applications to business, AIs will continue to grow more sophisticated and be given more and more responsibility that used to belong to humans.

Some believe this is a positive development. "It's well documented that we humans make mistakes," says a founder of an AI-driven trading fund. "For me, it's scarier to be relying on those human-based intuitions and justifications than relying on purely what the data and statistics are telling you."

As for Musk, he believes humanity needs to be proactive in **addressing the threats** posed by AI. "**Mark my words**: AI is far more dangerous than nukes. Far. So why do we have no regulatory oversight? This is insane."

(Adapted from *interestingengineering.com*)

☞ **Notes**

- **Elon Musk**: He is a South African-born American entrepreneur who cofounded the electronic-payment firm PayPal and formed SpaceX, maker of launch vehicles and spacecraft. He was also one of the first significant investors in, as well as chief executive officer of, the electric car manufacturer Tesla.
- **SpaceX**: It is an American aerospace company founded in 2002 that helped usher in the era of commercial spaceflight. It was the first private company to successfully launch and return a spacecraft from Earth orbit and the first to launch a crewed spacecraft and dock it with the International Space Station. Headquarters are in Hawthorne, California.
- **Stephen Hawking**: He was an English theoretical physicist whose theory of exploding black holes drew upon both relativity theory and quantum mechanics. He also worked with space-time singularities.

Opinion sharing

(a) Do you think technology accelerates the concentration of wealth? Why?

(b) Is technology contributing to increased inequality in education? Give reasons.
(c) Is modern technology a job destroyer or job creator? Give reasons.
(d) Which jobs are less likely to be taken over by machines? Why?
(e) Do we control technology or does technology control us? Why?

Reference Words and Expressions

redeploy	重新部署,再次有效利用
obsolete	过时的,淘汰的
redundant	多余的,被裁减的
demoralizing	使泄气的
lower-skilled / higher-skilled	较低技能的,较高技能的
semi-automated / fully-automated	半自动化的,全自动化的
unpredictability	难以预见性
retrain	再培训
customize	(按顾客要求)定制
ethicist	伦理学家
gene-edit	基因编辑

worsen social inequality	加剧社会不平等
widen socio-economic gaps	扩大社会、经济差距
aggravate social and economic stress	加剧社会、经济压力
create a skill gap	形成技能差距
drive regional polarization	驱动区域两极化
exert uneven impacts	产生不均衡影响
boost overall economic output	提高整体经济产出
invade the workforce	入侵劳动力市场
job displacement	裁员,工作位移
delegate mundane tasks to a robot	将单调的任务委派给机器人
automate repetitive or arduous tasks	使重复、艰巨的任务自动化
live in the most deprived areas	生活在最贫困的地区
AI-driven algorithm	由人工智能驱动的算法
a handful of tech giants	几个科技巨头
process large chunks of data	处理大量数据
augment human activities	加强人类活动
caution against policymakers	告诫政策制定者
defining challenge	决定性的挑战
ready oneself for the upheaval ahead	为即将到来的巨变做好准备
address the threats posed by...	应对来自……的威胁

act human	像人一样行动
hold a human consciousness	持有人类意识
empathy and sympathy	移情和同情
become an existential threat	变成一个生存威胁
evaluate the morality of its actions	评估其行为的道德性
from a human standpoint	从人类的角度来看
consensus on ethical principles	就道德原则达成共识
be ethically responsible	在道德上负责任的
prevent genetic disorders	预防遗传性疾病
lose diversity and individuality	失去多样性和个体性
trigger ethical debates	引发伦理争论
push ethical boundaries	挑战道德底线

Speaking Activities

Brainstorm

Robotization

Economists analyzed long-term trends around the uptake of automation in the workplace, noting that the number of robots in use worldwide increased threefold over the past two decades. Robots are expected to take over more than 20 million manufacturing jobs worldwide by 2030, extending a trend of worsening social inequality while boosting overall economic output, a new study shows.

(Adapted from *cnbc. com*)

(a) If you were a policymaker, would you slow the adoption of robotic technology?
(b) What could be done to help the workers who are affected by job automation?

Discussion

GMO

Genetically modified organism (GMO) refers to any organism whose DNA has been modified using genetic engineering technology. With this biotechnology, you can customize your offspring by having the opportunity to choose which genetic trait your unborn child should possess.

(Adapted from *newscientist. com*)

(a) Would you choose to genetically engineer your baby if possible? Why?
(b) What would happen if genetic engineering was only available to the wealthy?

Interview

Should Self-driving Cars Have Ethics?
In the not-too-distant future, fully autonomous vehicles will drive our streets. These cars will need to make split-second decisions to avoid endangering lives — both inside and outside of the vehicles. But self-driving technology presents vast ethical challenges: In face of an accident, should it spare humans over animals? Spare the lives of many over the few? Spare the young over the old?

(Adapted from *npr. org*)

Scenario: A crash took place between a self-driving car with two passengers and a traditional car with a driver only. The local news is going to interview the people involved in this accident:

— the driver in the traditional car
— two passengers in the self-driving car
— the seller of the self-driving car
— the developer of self-driving technology
— witnesses
— a car insurance broker
— a traffic policeman

Work in groups. One of you is the interviewer, others roleplay the above listed interviewees. After the interview, the interviewer summarizes the main ideas of the interviewees. Your interview may cover the following aspects:

(a) Who is to be blamed in this accident? Why?
(b) Should we customize traffic rules for self-driving cars? Why?
(c) Would you use a self-driving car? Why?

B2. 2 Privacy and Security

The following two passages focus on the ethical dilemmas that technology creates in our privacy and security. Read them and share your opinions according to the questions. Try to seek diverse perspectives and don't confine yourself to the reference words and expressions given.

Passage One

Ethical Issues of Internet Privacy

Bobby Schnabel

Internet privacy is a major concern today. It has raised certain ethical issues. Advertisers track your web activities and intrude on your privacy. Your online transactions, emails and social networking profiles are scanned, thus invading your online privacy. There could be valid reasons for this. But is this ethical? The Internet privacy needs of users should be catered to. And we cannot forget ethics. This article talks about the ethical issues of Internet privacy.

Think of this

If all the information accessed or shared over the Internet by a user is gathered from multiple sources (like his social networking profile, browsing habits, money transactions, etc.) and compiled, it can give you an almost complete picture of the kind of person he is.

Technology makes it possible to view all the information that is being exchanged over the web. It is of help against threats to web security and in protecting users from **security breaches.** But the same can be used to **disclose confidential information** for the wrong reasons, thus invading user privacy on the Internet. This gives rise to ethical issues surrounding the protection of critical information from **unauthorized access.** Internet privacy is the control you have over what information about yourself or your online activities you wish to disclose.

Internet privacy and ethics

Invasion of Internet privacy can be avoided with the strict implementation of privacy laws. But every act cannot be classified as legal or illegal. For example, an advertiser monitoring the online habits of web users to **target potential customers** is not illegal. But ethics dictate the extent to which network activity should be monitored. Network administrators in companies need to monitor **traffic to their server**, which includes tracking the Internet use by employees. It's ethics that draw the line between ensuring network security and breaching user privacy.

Online transactions

When shopping online, you share your credit card number or bank account details on the **shopping portal.** There is a potential of these details being used unethically or for **fraudulent purposes.** Online retailers collect data about your online behavior and use it in **user profiling.** Their intention is to make shopping recommendations and offers that **suit your taste and budget.** But is it ethical to track you without your consent?

While carrying out banking transactions online, you share details about your finances with the bank. **Malicious users** may obtain this information **by unethical means** and use it to their advantage. For the same reason, some are skeptical about banking or shopping online.

Government and other agencies

The government holds a lot of important data about people. The degree of access the government has to citizens' personal records raises ethical issues in information privacy. Using the records responsibly and maintaining their confidentiality is a prime duty of the government agencies.

There are many other organizations that store personal details and other critical information of their users. They include banks, medical facilities, educational institutes and companies that maintain employee records.

It is the duty of these agencies to take measures against the manipulation or unethical use of these records. Those involved in managing this information should be moral enough to not make any illegitimate or wrong use of it.

Social networking websites and privacy

Through **status updates** on social networking websites, you let everyone know of your location, and possibly some details about your personal life. You upload photos, your personal information, professional details, etc., onto your social networking profile. Technically, the social network owns the data you upload. This raises the ethical issue of whether these websites should store or use your information, and for what purposes. Even after an account is deleted, its details remain with the website. Do they permanently delete the records of deleted user accounts? Is the storing of records ethical?

Some users prefer anonymity when using the Internet. Is it ethically right to allow this? While it caters to the privacy needs of some users, it may endanger Internet use for others. Those involved in **cyberstalking** and hacking often use the Internet anonymously.

Internet cookies

Simply put, cookies are pieces of text sent by a server (website) to a browser and stored on your computer for future use. They are of use by the website or advertisers to track your preferences and serve you with information **tailored to your needs.** But cookies raise a privacy concern as they can be used by hackers too.

Advertisers use third-party cookies to track your visits to different domains, thus tracking your web preferences in general. Ethical issues arise when websites do not **notify** you of third-party cookies being used. It can damage your trust in the website.

How users are responsible

One common scenario where Internet privacy is **at stake**, rather is put to risk by the users themselves, is when they disclose personal details on websites without much thought. Be it posting your life's events on social networking websites or sharing personal details via emails; be it banking online or **accepting lucrative offers** on the Internet; it's you who agrees to share personal information, thus inviting an invasion of privacy.

The effort to ensure Internet privacy should start at the user's end. Choice of the right operating system (one with optimum security features), wise decisions on what information should or should not be disclosed when online and learning to identify trustworthy sources from the unreliable ones are keys to protect your privacy during Internet use.

Many are of the view that when on the web, you are connected to the world, and nothing of what you share on this platform can remain private. They think that there is no such concept as Internet privacy in the true sense. However, there are others who advocate the need of privacy on the Internet, and even prefer **anonymity** while using it. Complete anonymity is not the intent of Internet privacy. It rather intends to achieve controlled disclosure of critical information. Allowing the effective sharing of data while safeguarding personally identifiable or other confidential information is the real challenge. Visibility on the Internet is both good and bad. It allows easy transactions and exchange of information, but blurs the very idea of privacy. Also, the protection of privacy is of no use if Internet ethics are put at stake.

(Adapted from *coursera.org*)

☞**Notes**

- **cyberstalking**: It refers to a criminal practice where an individual uses Internet to systematically harass or threaten someone.
- **at stake**: It means being in danger of being lost.
- **anonymity**: It refers to the situation in which someone's name is not given or known.

Passage Two

The Surveillance Conundrum: Security vs. Privacy

Staff Writer

It's well documented that the U. K. is one of the most surveilled countries in the world. The average urban dweller is likely to be captured by 300 **CCTV** cameras a day, with the U. K. home to an estimated six million devices (excluding **body-worn video**, dash-cams, helmet-cams and drones).

Recent terrorist attacks have underlined the importance of surveillance — prompting the U. K. Government to **pass a controversial act** which grants security services widespread surveillance abilities: the permission to hack into computers, the mass interception and collection of communications data, and the acquisition of personal data sets from companies and organizations.

The Investigatory Powers Act, which became a law in November 2016 and was enforced shortly after, has been fiercely challenged by civil rights activists and has once again been **brought into the spotlight** concerning the delicate balance between surveillance and privacy.

Most people understand the importance of surveillance in creating a safe society — surveys suggest mass public support of CCTV in a public space. However, people aren't always prepared to give up their privacy to facilitate tighter monitoring of criminals.

Speaking to *The Telegraph*, Sir John Sawers, ex-Director of the Secret Intelligence Service (MI6), explained: "There is a dilemma because the general public, politicians and technology companies, to some extent, want us to be able to monitor the activities of terrorists and other evil-doers but they don't want their own activities to be open to any such monitoring."

It's not only public bodies that are upping surveillance in the U. K. — growth in civil deployment is also expected to rise as organizations and individuals look to protect themselves and the general public. In particular, these private sector firms are increasingly turning to body-worn video — following the Metropolitan Police's lead, who are enjoying various benefits from deploying the devices.

However, before an organization adopts body-worn video, they need to weigh up the pros and cons of using means of surveillance, which will help them decide whether it will prove a sound investment.

ADVANTAGES

Deter crime

This is the biggest and the most obvious benefit of surveillance. The mere sight of a camera — body-worn video or otherwise — causes them to **think twice before acting**. So, for organizations that deal with people in situations where emotions are heightened, there is a clear advantage in being able to tell subjects that they are being filmed — usually, their behaviour will reflect this and a possible crime will not be committed.

Gather evidence

Surveillance camera **footage** provides organizations with strong evidence when a crime has been committed, which can be handed over to the police, allowing them to make a case for prosecution. This will allow organizations to claim for damage or losses in the event of a crime against them, while ensuring that justice is done. High-quality camera footage is particularly helpful when an eyewitness may have forgotten a certain important detail or may be providing with an inaccurate account of what really transpired.

Protect reputation

Footage from security cameras can help organizations make correct and fair decisions when **settling disputes**. Accusing the wrong person of a misdemeanour can impact an organization's reputation and even result in a loss of custom. Similarly, not having the means to gather video evidence could make prosecution difficult in the event of a crime, which may cause an organization to get a reputation for failing in its duty to protect its customers. Meanwhile, incorrect, inappropriate or fabricated claims made by customers or other authorities can also **be cleared up** through video footage.

DISADVANTAGES

Privacy implications

People may **object to** their face being captured on camera, which is enough in itself to cause a disagreement and a potentially unsavoury situation. Often, objecting citizens will cite an "**invasion of privacy**", so organizations will need to know the laws in this area so that they don't fall foul of any legislation.

Cost, data implications

Surveillance cameras are coming down in price, but organizations will likely have to buy a number of them so that they are fully covered, making them a costly expense. The cameras will also need to be maintained to ensure that they continue to work effectively, with any data or footage managed according to data protection laws.

The advantages clearly outweigh the disadvantages. Whether an organization adopts some means of surveillance depends on which argument wins out of the privacy vs. security debate.

(Adapted from *memberportal.bsigroup.com*)

☞**Notes**

- **CCTV**: It is an abbreviation for closed-circuit television, a system that sends television signals to a limited number of screens, and is often used in shops and public places to prevent crime.
- **footage**: It is the total number of running feet of motion-picture film used (as for a scene or subject); the material contained on such footage.

Opinion sharing

(a) How does information leaking affect your personal life?

(b) Is it acceptable for companies to secretly collect and sell data from a user? Why?

(c) Should employees be monitored at workplace by live surveillance cameras? Why?
(d) What is your view on in-home security cameras?
(e) When should we give up personal privacy for public security? Give reasons.

Reference Words and Expressions

breach	破坏,违犯
transparency	透明度
authentification	认证
anonymity	匿名
geotag	标出地理位置
alias	别名,昵称
cybersecurity	网络安全
hot-button issue	敏感话题
trade privacy for security	用隐私换取安全
make a trade-off between A and B	在两者之间权衡利弊
infringe individual privacy right	侵犯个人隐私权
breach user privacy	侵犯用户隐私
incursion on one's privacy	个人隐私侵犯
violate civil rights	侵犯公民权利
full-body scanner	全身扫描仪
disclose confidential information	泄露秘密信息
gather data without consent	未经同意收集数据
feed data directly into the Internet	直接传送数据至因特网
enforce real-name registration online	实行网络实名制
identification fraud	身份欺诈
verify identity	确认身份
forbid anonymous online posts	禁止匿名在线发帖
prevent electronic rumor-mongering	预防网上散布谣言
disrupt social order	扰乱社会秩序
violence and slander	暴力和诽谤
create fake profiles	创建虚假简介
alter privacy settings	更改隐私设置
unselect an option	取消选项
denied access	不可访问/不可进入
beef up security	加强安保
spy on citizens	监视市民
by unethical means	借助不道德手段

deface democracy	玷污民主
an all-purpose tool	万能工具
real-time tracking	实时追踪
curb mobile phone crimes	控制手机犯罪
enhance public safety	增强公共安全
avoid the perils of misuse	避免滥用的危险
make surveillance cheap and invisible	让监视变得廉价且隐形
undergo a facial-recognition scan	进行面部识别扫描
yield mixed results	结果好坏参半

Speaking Activities

Individual talk

Airport Body Scanners

A regular part of traveling today is going through the airport body scanner before boarding your flight. These scanners have been a source of much controversy. On the one hand, we want to feel safe and confident in security measures. On the other, we don't want to wait in lengthy queues emptying our pockets, taking off coats and shoes. And we don't want to feel like our privacy right is being infringed.

(Adapted from *bustle.com*)

Can you list any other cases when privacy and security might contradict?

Discussion

Moments on social media platforms are a cool idea. Numerous people like posting or sharing things on their Moments. If you lead an interesting life, they can be a nice way to share that with your friends. However, Moments might pose danger to your privacy and security at the same time.

(a) Do you often post Moments on your social media platform? Why?
(b) Would you set who can view your Moments and who cannot? Why?
(c) What privacy problems might Moments cause?
(d) How can you cope with the above-mentioned problems?

Debate

Many cybersecurity experts advocate that real-name registration should be enforced to regulate online comments. Only those who have their real name and identification information registered will be able to comment on Internet platforms.

Topic for debate: To be anonymous or not to be? Should you use your real name on the Internet?

B3. Extensive Reading

Top 9 Ways Artificial Intelligence Prevents Fraud

Louis Columbus

The future of AI-based fraud prevention relies on the combination of supervised and unsupervised machine learning. Supervised machine learning excels at examining events, factors, and trends from the past. Historical data trains supervised machine learning models to find patterns not discernable with rules or predictive analytics. Unsupervised machine learning is adept at finding anomalies, interrelationships, and valid links between emerging factors and variables. Combining both unsupervised and supervised machine learning defines the future of AI-based fraud prevention and is the foundation of the top nine ways AI prevents fraud.

AI is re-defining fraud prevention from relying only on past experiences to taking into account emerging activities, behaviors, and trends in transaction anomalies. Before AI, fraud prevention systems would rely on rules alone, which excel at analyzing past fraud patterns without providing insights into the future. By combining supervised learning algorithms trained on historical data with unsupervised learning, digital businesses gain a greater level of acuity and clarity about the relative risk of customers' behaviors. Decisions to accept or reject payment, stop fraudulent activity to limit chargebacks and reduce risk are all possible now, thanks to AI.

AI makes it possible to detect fraud attacks in real-time versus having to wait six or eight weeks until chargebacks start coming in. AI's ability to detect fraud attacks in less than a second using advanced AI-based rating technologies like Omniscore is the future of fraud management. When a digital business relies on structured learning and rules alone, new attacks are very difficult to catch. Chargebacks show up 6 to 8 weeks after the fraud has taken place, and digital businesses rush to update their rules engines. By balancing supervised and unsupervised learning, AI alleviates the need always to play catch-up to online fraud.

It's now possible to thwart more sophisticated, nuanced abuse attacks including referring a friend abuse, promotion abuse, or seller collusion in a marketplace. Rules engines and predictive analytics can scale only so far in thwarting fraud attempts. Digital businesses will often revert to stricter, controlling standards for transaction approvals if they have been burned by fraud before. The result is a bad user experience. By having an AI-based fraud prevention system do the work of evaluating historical data and anomalies, customer experiences can stay more positive, and the more sophisticated nuanced abuse attacks can be stopped.

AI provides fraud analysts with real-time risk scores and greater insight into where best to set threshold scores to maximize sales and minimize fraud losses. The best fraud analysts have an intuitive sense of when transaction patterns are legitimate or not. With AI, a fraud analyst receives a 360-degree view of transactions for the first time, having the benefit of seeing historical data in context. Adding in anomaly detection and insights into real-time activity using unsupervised machine learning, fraud analysts can instantly validate or redefine their decision regarding threshold levels, managing risk well.

AI enables digital businesses to gain greater control over chargeback rates, decline rates, and operational costs so that business objectives can be achieved. One of the most valuable aspects of an AI-based fraud prevention platform is its ability to instantly customize and change business outcomes specific to the entire business, separate products lines, departments, and selling seasons. Digital businesses are relying on the combination of supervised and unsupervised machine learning to attain greater levels of agility, speed, and time-to-market, with AI-based fraud prevention systems being foundational to that effort.

AI enables digital businesses selling virtual goods, including gaming, to provide a more consistent, high-quality user experience on a 24/7 basis. Online games have exponentially grown in popularity over the last five years with online gaming platforms often having over 250 million customers worldwide. Game platform providers want as many people as possible on the platforms to drive advertising, subscription, upsell, and cross-sell revenue. For game platform providers to succeed, they need to provide an immediate, highly responsive purchase experience. Instead of forcing their customers or fans to go through verification, they can assign a risk score to the transaction and fulfill the purchase request in seconds. AI makes it possible for gamers to buy the coins or tokens they need when they need them to keep playing. AI-based fraud prevention systems make it possible to immediately accept the transactions while still staying within the chargeback thresholds.

AI reduces the friction customers experience by helping merchants easily approve online purchases and reduce false positives. One of the paradoxes fraud analysts face is what level to set the decline rate at. Instead of having to make an educated guess, fraud analysts can turn to AI-based scoring techniques like Omniscore that combine the strengths of supervised and unsupervised learning. AI-based fraud scores like Omniscore reduces false positives, which is a major source of friction with customers. All this translates into fewer manual escalations, declines, and an overall more positive customer experience.

Staying in compliance with internal business policies, those from regulatory agencies and agreements with distribution partners is where AI-based fraud prevention is contributing today. Many digital businesses have internal business policies regarding the sales of specific products to specific countries based on distribution and reseller agreements. Businesses competing in high technology industries need to stay in compliance with export regulations that protect key technologies as well. AI-based scoring and fraud prevention are extensively used to keep businesses in compliance.

AI enables low-margin businesses and product lines to stay profitable by controlling chargebacks levels that have a direct impact on margins. E-commerce businesses thrive on offering price, availability, and a positive and seamless customer experience. Many sacrifice gross margins for greater scale and more transactions. The challenge is staying profitable while attracting new customers whose purchase history is not part of the supervised learning history of their fraud systems. That's where an AI-based approach that incorporates both unsupervised and supervised learning pays off from a gross margin standpoint.

(Adapted from *forbes. com*)

References

Michael Fett. Technology, Health and Health Care. *Occasional Papers*. Retrieved from https://www.health.gov.au/internet/main/Publishing.nsf/Content/DA8177ED1A80D332CA257BF0001B08EE/$File/ocpahfsv5.pdf on March 19th, 2021.

Ann Pietrangelo. (2019). How Does Technology Affect Your Health? *Healthline*. Retrieved from https://www.healthline.com/health/negative-effects-of-technology on March 19th, 2021.

Walden University. How Is Modern Technology Affecting Human Brains? *Walden University*. Retrieved from https://www.waldenu.edu/online-masters-programs/ms-in-developmental-psychology/resource/how-is-modern-technology-affecting-human-development on March 19th, 2021.

Elaine Cox. (2019). Is Technology the Health Care Wave of the Future? *U. S. News*. Retrieved from https://health.usnews.com/health-care/for-better/articles/pros-and-cons-of-technology-in-health-care on March 19th, 2021.

Rahul Parikh. (2018). AI Can't Replace Doctors but Make Them Better. *MIT Technology Review*. Retrieved from https://www.technologyreview.com/2018/10/23/139414/ai-cant-replace-doctors-but-it-can-make-them-better on March 19th, 2021.

George Michelsen Foy. (2017). Is GPS Dangerous to Your Health? *Daily Beast*. Retrieved from https://www.thedailybeast.com/is-gps-dangerous-to-your-health on March 19th, 2021.

Expert Panel. (2020). Technology Causes Ethical Dilemmas. *Forbes*. Retrieved from https://www.forbes.com/sites/forbestechcouncil/2020/07/09/15-ethical-crises-in-technology-that-have-industry-leaders-concerned/?sh=45d728dc7be9 on March 19th, 2021.
Kentaro Toyama. (2015). Can Technology Offer Solutions to Inequality? *USA Today*. Retrieved from https://www.usatoday.com/story/tech/2015/05/29/kentaro-toyama-guest-column-inequality-zuckerberg-braff-clinton/28034093 on March 19th, 2021.
John Loeffler. (2019). AIs Continue to Act in Unpredictable Ways, Should We Panic? *Interesting Engineering*. Retrieved from https://interestingengineering.com/ais-continue-to-act-in-unpredictable-ways-should-we-panic on March 19th, 2021.
Bobby Schnabel. Ethical Issues of Internet Privacy. *Coursera*. Retrieved from https://www.coursera.org/lecture/ethical-issues-data-science/privacy-part-2-6gS9H on March 19th, 2021.
Staff Writer. (2017). The Surveillance Conundrum: Security vs. Privacy. *Bsi*. Retrieved from https://memberportal.bsigroup.com/public/2017/july/the-surveillance-conundrum-security-vs-privacy on March 19th, 2021.
Kendra Cherry. (2020). Multitasking. *Very Well Mind*. Retrieved from https://www.verywellmind.com/multitasking-2795003 on March 19th, 2021.
S. Randall Hood. (2018). Surgical Robots. *McGowan, Hood & Felder, LLC*. Retrieved from https://www.mcgowanhood.com/2018/09/13/da-vinci-surgical-robots-have-been-linked-to-at-least-144-deaths on March 19th, 2021.
Nurses Are Here to Stay. *All Nurses*. Retrieved from https://allnurses.com/do-think-nurses-will-replaced-t527614/ on March 19th, 2021.
Chloe Taylor. (2019). Robotization. *CNBC*. Retrieved from https://www.cnbc.com/2019/06/26/robots-could-take-over-20-million-jobs-by-2030-study-claims.html on March 19th, 2021.
Michael Le Page. (2019). GMO. *New Scientist*. Retrieved from https://www.newscientist.com/question/genetically-modified-organism on March 19th, 2021.
Laurel Wamsley. (2018). Should Self-driving Cars Have Ethics? *NPR*. Retrieved from https://www.npr.org/2018/10/26/660775910/should-self-driving-cars-have-ethics on March 19th, 2021.
Brandi Neal. (2019). Airport Body Scanners. *Bustle*. Retrieved from https://www.bustle.com/p/what-do-body-scanners-in-airports-detect-heres-why-theyll-sometimes-flag-random-things-15770621 on March 19th, 2021.
Louis Columbus. (2019). Top 9 Ways Artificial Intelligence Prevents Fraud. *Forbes*. Retrieved from https://www.forbes.com/sites/louiscolumbus/2019/07/09/top-9-ways-artificial-intelligence-prevents-fraud/?sh=1c6d622814b4 on March 19th, 2021.

Unit 4 Environment

Part A Pollution

A1. Introduction

What Is Pollution?

Pollution occurs when an amount of any substance or any form of energy is put into the environment at a rate faster than it can be dispersed or safely stored. The term "pollution" can refer to both artificial and natural materials that are created, consumed and discarded in an unsustainable manner.

Although environmental pollution can be caused by natural events such as forest fires and active volcanoes, use of the word "pollution" generally implies that the contaminants have an anthropogenic source — that is, a source created by human activities. Pollution has accompanied humankind ever since groups of people first congregated and remained for a long time in any one place. Indeed, ancient human settlements are frequently recognized by their wastes — shell mounds and rubble heaps, for instance. Pollution was not a serious problem as long as there was enough space available for each individual or group. However, with the establishment of permanent settlements by great numbers of people, pollution became a problem, and it has remained one ever since.

Types of Pollution

As stated before, there are different types of pollution, which are either caused by natural events (like forest fires) or by man-made activities (like cars, factories, nuclear wastes, etc.) These are further classified into the following types of pollution.

Air pollution refers to the release of harmful contaminants (chemicals, toxic gases, particulates, biological molecules, etc.) into the earth's atmosphere. These contaminants are quite detrimental and, in some cases, pose serious health issues. Some causes that contribute to air pollution are:

- Burning fossil fuels
- Mining operations
- Exhaust gases from industries and factories

The effects of air pollution vary based on the kind of pollutant. But generally, the impact of air pollution ranges from:

- Increased risk of respiratory illness and cardiovascular problems
- Increased risk of skin diseases
- May increase the risk of cancer
- Global warming
- Acid rain
- Ozone depletion
- Hazards to wildlife

Among the other types of pollution, air pollution is theorized to have a planet-wide implication. Scientists have even speculated an apocalypse-like scenario where air pollution if left unchecked, can bring about an extreme form of global warming called the runaway greenhouse effect. Though this is purely speculative, it is a phenomenon that has already occurred on Venus.

Water pollution is said to occur when toxic pollutants and particulate matter are introduced into water bodies such as lakes, rivers and seas. These contaminants are generally introduced by human activities like improper sewage treatment and oil spills. However, even natural processes such as eutrophication can cause water pollution.

Other significant causes of water pollution include:

- Dumping solid wastes in water bodies
- Disposing untreated industrial sewage into water bodies
- Human and animal wastes
- Agricultural runoff containing pesticides and fertilizers

The effects of water pollution are very pronounced in our environment. Furthermore, toxic chemicals can bioaccumulate in living beings, and these chemicals can travel their way up the food chain, ultimately reaching humans.

Among the other types of pollution, water pollution has a more disastrous consequence on humans. For instance, in 1932, a grave case of water pollution incapacitated the inhabitants of an entire city in Japan with neurological diseases and mental illness for many decades. However, the immediate cause was not apparent but was eventually attributed to acute mercury poisoning. Methylmercury was dumped into the surrounding bay and had ultimately bioaccumulated inside the fish. The local population then consumed these fish, and this resulted in the manifestation of ill-effects and neurological diseases.

Soil pollution, also called soil contamination, refers to the degradation of land due to the presence of chemicals or other man-made substances in the soil. The xenobiotic substances alter the natural composition of soil and affect it negatively. These can drastically impact life directly or indirectly. For instance, any toxic chemicals present in the soil will get absorbed by the plants. Since plants are producers in an environment, it gets passed up through the food chain. Compared to the other types of pollution, the effects of soil pollution are a little more obscured, but their implications are very noticeable.

Some of the common causes of soil pollution are:

- Improper industrial waste disposal
- Oil Spills
- Acid rain which is caused by air pollution
- Mining activities
- Intensive farming and agrochemicals (like fertilizers and pesticides)
- Industrial accidents

The effects of soil pollution are numerous. Specific wastes, such as radioactive waste become particularly hazardous when they are not well-contained. A well-documented example is a nuclear accident in Chernobyl, which has left an area of 2,600 km^2 uninhabitable for several thousand years.

Other effects of soil pollution include:

- Loss of soil nutrients, which renders the soil unfit for agriculture
- Impacts the natural flora and fauna residing in the soil
- Degrades vegetation due to the increase of salinity of the soil
- Toxic dust (such as silica dust) can cause respiratory problems or even lung cancer

Noise pollution refers to the excessive amount of noise in the surrounding that disrupts the natural balance. Usually, it is man-made, though certain natural calamities like volcanoes can contribute to noise pollution.

In general, any sound which is over 85 decibels is considered to be detrimental. Also, the duration an individual is exposed has an impact on their health. A normal conversation is around 60 decibels, and a jet taking off is around 150 decibels. Consequently, noise pollution is more obvious than the other types of pollution.

Noise pollution has several contributors, which include:

- Industry-oriented noises such as heavy machines, mills, factories, etc.
- Transportation noises from vehicles, airplanes, etc.
- Construction noises
- Noises from social events (loudspeakers, firecrackers, etc.)
- Household noises (such as mixers, TVs, washing machines, etc.)

Noise pollution has now become very common due to dense urbanization and industrialization. Noise pollution can bring about adverse effects such as:

- Hearing loss
- Tinnitus
- Sleeping disorders
- Hypertension (high BP)
- Communication problems

Besides these 4 types of pollution, other types exist such as light pollution, thermal pollution and radioactive pollution. The latter is much rarer than other types, but it is the deadliest.

(Adapted from *britannica.com*; *byjus.com*)

A2. Passage Reading

A2.1 Life-threatening Pollution

The following two passages focus on life-related pollution. Read and give your opinions according to the questions. Try to seek diverse perspectives and don't confine yourself to the reference words and expressions given.

Passage One

Scientists Determine Cause of London's 1952 "Killer Fog"

Kacey Deamer

London may be known for its **drizzly** weather, but in 1952 the city's **quintessential fog** cover turned **deadly**, and no one knew exactly why — until now.

For five days in December 1952, a fog that contained **pollutants enveloped all of London.** By the time the dense fog cover **lifted**, more than 150,000 people had been hospitalized and at least 4,000 people had died. Researchers now estimate that the total death count was likely more than 12,000 people, as well as thousands of animals. Despite its **lethal nature**, the exact cause and nature of the killer fog has largely remained a mystery. Recently, a team of researchers has determined the likely reasons for its formation.

Researchers have for a long time connected **emissions from burning coal** with the killer fog, but the specific chemical processes that led to the deadly mix of pollution and fog were not fully understood. To determine what turned the fog into a killer, an international team of scientists from China, the U. S. and the U. K. recreated the fog in a lab using results from laboratory experiments and atmospheric measurements from Beijing and Xi'an.

Study lead author Renyi Zhang, an atmospheric scientist at Texas A&M University, said that sulfate was a big contributor to the deadly London fog. Sulfuric acid particles, which formed from the sulfur dioxide that **was released from** the burning of coal, were also a **component** of the fog. The question was, how did sulfur dioxide get turned into sulfuric acid?

"Our results showed that this process was facilitated by nitrogen dioxide, another co-product of coal burning, and occurred initially on natural fog," Zhang said in a statement. "Another key aspect in the **conversion** of sulfur dioxide to sulfate is that it produces acidic particles, which subsequently inhibits this process."

The natural fog contained larger particles, Zhang explained, with the smaller acidic particles evenly distributed throughout. When those fog particles evaporated, an **acidic-haze** was left covering the city.

The 1952 killer fog led to the creation of the Clean Air Act, which the British Parliament passed in 1956. Researchers still consider it the worst air pollution event in European history.

(Adapted from *cbsnews.com*)

☞**Notes**

The Clean Air Act: The 1952 London smog disaster is thought to have claimed as many as 12,000 lives. Following this tragedy, the government passed the Clean Air Act of 1956. This for the first time regulated both domestic and industrial smoke emissions. Historians widely considered the Clean Air Act a milestone in environmental protection. The legislation included powers to establish smokeless zones, and provided subsidies to householders to convert to cleaner fuels (smokeless solid fuel, gas and electricity). But this energy transition did not happen overnight. It took around 3 decades, and another Clean Air Act in 1968 was passed to deal with slow-moving local authorities, before smoke control programs were finally completed.

By the 1980s the skies had cleared — improving health and quality of life in the cities of the world's first industrial nation. But the problem is not eradicated. Today filthy air is the cause of up to 36,000 early deaths in the U. K. each year. (Adapted from *friendsoftheearth. uk*)

Passage Two

Japan to Release Radioactive Fukushima Water into Ocean

Nishan Degnarain

The new Prime Minister of Japan, Yoshihide Suga, is facing additional **international pressure** over the weekend, amid reports that Japan will be accelerating plans to **dump** millions of gallons of **radioactive water** directly into the ocean.

Reports have been widely circulated among Japan's leading news agency and across international media that suggest the decision has already been taken by the new Japanese government, and will be publicly communicated later this month.

Over 1. 2 million tons of **radioactive cooling water** from the Fukushima Nuclear Plant will **be released**. While the water will be treated, it will still be radioactive. 170 tons of new radioactive wastewater is generated each day and is stored in 1000 specially designed tanks.

Environmentalists and local fishermen have been urging the Japanese government to reconsider this option, after almost a decade trying to build back their reputation around the plant, where **elevated radioactive levels** can still be detected.

South Korea still bans all seafood imports from this part of Japan, and has held urgent talks with Japanese counterparts to try and find a more measured approach to managing the Fukushima water crisis that would not **risk the environment or human health**.

The outrage over these plans comes just three weeks after Prime Minister Suga personally visited the Fukushima plant, on September 26.

It follows a series of policy announcements by Japan that raises questions about how effective the country is **a sustainable steward of the ocean** amid the global climate and **biodiversity crisis.** In 2019, Japan withdrew from the International Whaling Commission to begin commercial whaling. At the UN shipping regulator, the IMO, Japan chairs the influential Environment Committee and has consistently pushed for much lower emission and pollution standards for its powerful shipping lobby.

To cool radioactive fuel cores at the damaged Fukushima nuclear plant, Japan had pumped 1.2 million tons of water through the rods and this water became contaminated with radioactive tritium. Once used for cooling, this radioactive tritium cannot be removed, so the water was placed into storage.

Japan is now **running out of space** as it rushes to fully **decommission the nuclear plant.** The clean-up has already cost the Japanese utility owner, Tokyo Electric Power Company (TEPCO), $200 billion. According to the Japanese Ministry of Environment, its tanks will be full by 2022.

Japanese ministers under former Prime Minister Shinzo Abe's government had been pushing for the dumping of radioactive waste in the ocean for years. Last year, Japan's environment minister said that the only solution was to "release it into the ocean and dilute it".

"There are no other options." he said.

(Adapted from *forbes.com*)

Opinion sharing

(a) Who do you think is more responsible for air pollution, the government or individuals? Explain.
(b) What are the possible causes of sea pollution?
(c) What are the possible consequences of sea pollution?
(d) Share some specific cases of pollution around you.
(e) Choose one of the cases and think about how you can deal with the problem.

Reference Words and Expressions

particles	颗粒
methane	甲烷
chemicals	化学物质
prohibit	禁止

degrade	降解
unhealthy air	不健康的空气
decline in air quality	空气质量下降
increasing human consumption patterns	日益增加的人类消费模式
driven by population growth	受人口增长的驱动
common pollutants	常见的污染物
concentrations of pollutants	污染物浓度
indoor and outdoor air pollution	室内外空气污染
link to higher rates of cancer	与越来越高的癌症发病率相关
premature death	夭折，过早死亡
respiratory disease	呼吸系统疾病
pose health risks	造成健康风险
climate change	气候变化
extreme weather	极端天气
heat waves	热浪
increased greenhouse gases	不断增加的温室气体
negative impact	负面影响
emit carbon dioxide	排放二氧化碳
trap heat	蓄热
burning of fossil fuels	化石燃料的燃烧
deteriorating effects on ozone layer	对臭氧层的恶化影响
component of smog	雾霾成分
acid rain	酸雨
clean up smog-choked skies	清洗雾霾污染的天空
set emission standards	设定排放标准
improve air quality	提高空气质量
cleaner cooking options	更清洁的烹饪选择
curb global warming	遏制全球变暖
renewable energy	可再生能源
household garbage	生活垃圾
industrial waste	工业废物
plastics, rubber, leather and textile	塑料、橡胶、皮革和纺织品
organic material	有机材料
generate hazardous waste	产生有害废物
petroleum refining	石油精炼
pesticide manufacturing	农药生产
chemical production sewage	化工生产污水

excessive use of fertilizer	肥料的过度使用
sound reaches a harmful level	声音达到有害程度
artificial light	人造光
radioactive material concentration	放射性物质浓度
radioactive decay	放射性衰变
nuclear power plant accidents	核电站事故
nuclear missiles and atomic bombs	核导弹和原子弹

Speaking Activities

Individual talk

Talk about the air quality in your hometown. According to your observation, what might contribute to the good / bad air quality?

Read and discuss

Fireworks Ban

In recent years, there have been more legal restrictions on fireworks in terms of manufacture, selling and possession as well as individual use. People can only get firecrackers in designated shops and set off in restricted periods and zones.

The ban is looser in rural areas, and the tradition of setting off fireworks is widely kept, but there are truly a lot of problems. There are many accidents caused by firecracker explosions every year. During the Spring Festival, fire hazards are frequent, leading to damages and loss in different levels. In addition, the smog of firecrackers poses a threat to air quality.

(Adapted from *travelchinaguide. com*)

Topic for debate: Fireworks should be banned in urban areas in China.

Read and discuss

Garbage Sorting

Good news for our planet: the world's most populous country gets serious about tackling its waste problem. Forty-four days after Shanghai implemented what netizens called the most stringent and complex waste segregation regulations "in history", other Chinese cities want to speed up the cleaning up process too, because of the initial success of the "Shanghai model".

(Adapted from *cgtn. com*)

(a) How many types of garbage do you know?
(b) What made it so difficult for garbage sorting to be implemented?
(c) What positive impact can garbage sorting bring to our environment?

A2.2 Pollution-related Controversy

The following two passages focus on pollution-related controversy. Read and give your opinions according to the questions. Try to seek diverse perspectives and don't confine yourself to the reference words and expressions given.

Passage One

Which Is Worse for the Planet: Beef or Cars?

Jordyn Cormier

Cars are often used as the golden standard of environmental destruction. We know that our driving is hurtful to the environment. But, what about a burger? We don't instinctually **associate meat consumption with climate change**, but does the dark side of the meat industry **give cars a run for their money**? Which is actually worse — cows or cars?

Livestock emissions make up anywhere between 14.5 and 18 percent of total global greenhouse gas emissions. Comparably, the transportation sector is responsible for around 14 percent of emissions. By those numbers alone, our current system of meat production is extremely damaging. Perhaps more **looming**, however, is that while transportation creates CO_2, livestock farming is hugely responsible for producing methane. As you may know, methane is 23 times **more potent** when it comes to warming the planet.

Yes, driving cars is no good, but meat production is unexpectedly worse for the environment. Besides all of the fertilizer and cow waste products that release methane, meat unfortunately has to be transported in refrigerated trucks from feedlots to slaughterhouses to processing centers to your local grocery store. In this way, factory farming combines all of the harmful effects of driving an 18-wheeler.

The issue is that meat does not **appear as harmful upon cursory glance.** You can see emissions coming out of your old car and seeping into the atmosphere. You can't see emissions coming out of your hamburger. Although, if you could see cow farts, that'd be a different story, as they shouldn't be underestimated in their profound environmental impact. Buying grass-fed beef reduces entropic emissions (methane gas flatulence) in cows simply because their stomachs are designed to digest grass, not grains. So, small changes do make a difference.

If everyone enjoyed one meatless day a week — **a simple and easily accomplished request,** livestock emissions could be greatly reduced. Unfortunately, a rise in sustainable farming, while more humane and necessary, will not greatly alter the skyrocketing emissions caused by livestock. This is especially true since meat consumption is growing across the globe and projected to increase by around 70 percent by 2050. The only way to clean up our act is to change how we produce, consume and think about meat. We need to become less meat-centric as a whole.

Eating less meat is much **more easily accomplished** than converting our entire country's infrastructure to utilize renewable energy — although we still need to be moving in that direction. We can start eating less meat immediately. Consuming less meat is also one of the few tactics for reducing greenhouse emissions that actually costs the consumer less money. Private solar panels cost money. New, fuel efficient vehicles cost money. Eating less meat means you're potentially saving a little bit of money. It's something that we can all do.

Clearly, what we need is **a shift in mindset**. Meat consumption is deeply rooted and deeply held in many cultures, but it has become a dangerous obsession. It's like we are all sitting in a room steadily filling with smoke. It's clear that something is on fire, but no one else is doing anything, so we sit tight. But, if you were in that room alone and it started flooding with smoke, wouldn't you do something? Stop waiting for others to act. Make changes in your life to help the planet and others are sure to follow.

I don't believe that humans will ever stop eating meat. But it should be a priority to **practice moderation with our meat consumption**, if not for our collective health, then for the planet's.

(Adapted from *ecowatch.com*)

Passage Two

Environmental Impacts of Tourism

Oishimaya Sen Nag

Tourism is usually regarded as **a boon to a region's economy**. Tourism brings prosperity to the region and provides employment to the locals of the region. However, when tourism becomes **unsustainable in nature**, it can have disastrous consequences on the environment.

Air pollution

The movement of tourists from their home to the tourist destination involves transport via road, rail, or air, or a combination of these modes of transport. When a large number of tourists are involved, it invariably leads to a greater use of the transportation system. We all are aware of the fact that emissions from automobiles and airplanes are one of the biggest causes of air pollution. When a large number of tourists use these modes of transport to reach a particular attraction, it pollutes the air both locally and globally. Due to the rapid growth in international tourism, tourists now **account for** nearly 60% of air travel. In many places, buses or other vehicles **leave their motors running** to ensure that tourists return to comfortable air-conditioned vehicles. Such practices further pollute the air.

Noise pollution

Tourist destinations are often subject to significant noise pollution. Tourist vehicles entering and leaving natural areas create a lot of noise. Such noise is **the source of distress for wildlife.** Loud music played by tourists in forested areas also disturb the animals living in the area. Often, noise generated by tourist activities for long-term **alters the natural activity patterns of animals.**

Littering

Irresponsible tourists often litter the tourist spots visited by them. **Waste disposal** is a great problem in the natural environment. According to estimates, cruise ships in the Caribbean produce over 70, 000 tons of waste annually. If waste **is disposed of** irresponsibly in the sea, it can lead to the death of marine animals. Even the Mount Everest is not **free of human-generated waste.** Trekkers leave behind their oxygen cylinders, garbage, and camping equipment on the mountains and hills. Some trails in the Himalayas and the Andes have been nicknamed the "toilet paper trail" or the "Coca-Cola trail", referring to the garbage left behind on such trails.

Sewage

Rampant construction of tourist facilities like hotels, cafes, restaurants, etc. , in an area without proper arrangement for safe disposal of sewage, can lead to disastrous consequences. Wastewater carrying sewage from such areas often pollutes nearby water bodies. It can lead to the eutrophication of water bodies and the loss of the balance in aquatic ecosystems. Pollution of water bodies with sewage can also lead to health issues and even epidemics that can ultimately **wipe out** large populations of **aquatic flora and fauna** and also impact human health adversely.

Tourism and natural resources

When tourism is encouraged in an area with inadequate resources, it will have a negative impact on the ecosystem of the area. In such areas, the local flora and fauna might **be deprived of the resources needed** to sustain their lives. For example, large volumes of water are consumed to cater to the needs of the tourists, run hotels and swimming pools, maintain golf courses, etc. This can **degrade the quality of water** and decrease the volume of water that is available for the local population, plants and animals.

Tourism and physical degradation of the ecosystem

Every ecosystem works on a delicate natural balance. Every species in the ecosystem has a specific role to play in the system. However, tourism often disturbs this delicate balance and creates a great disaster in the ecosystem. When the tourist industry active in an area is completely **profit-minded**, it **pays little heed to** the needs of nature. For example, often hotels and resorts are built illegally very close to the beach or inside the core areas of forests. Large patches of natural vegetation need to be cleared to allow space for **the sprawling resorts** or hotels. As old tourist spots get degraded due to overuse by tourists, newer "upcoming" destinations with fewer crowds become the next favorite of tourists and the tourism industry. The same situation is repeated once more. **Unsustainable practices** by the tourism industry can thus lead to **deforestation**, **sand erosion**, **loss of species**, changes in sea currents and coastlines, destruction of habitats, etc.

(Adapted from *worldatlas. com*)

Opinion sharing

(a) Can you list some cases of over-consumption that cause pollution in your life? What could you do to avoid them?
(b) Increased population in cities leads to increased housing construction. How does it affect the urban environment?
(c) When you take a camping trip to the forest with your friends, what kind of pollution might be caused in the process?
(d) How can we deal with tourism pollution?
(e) Do you know any other pollution-related controversies? Please elaborate on one of them.

Reference Words and Expressions

recycle	回收
per capita	人均
deforestation	森林砍伐
produce greenhouse gas	产生温室气体
reduce reproduction	减少繁殖(生育)
changes in lifestyle	改变生活方式
use energy-efficient appliances	使用节能电器
add tons of carbon dioxide	增加成吨的二氧化碳
carbon emissions of individuals	个人碳排放
burgeoning population	蓬勃增长的人口

increasing global consumption of resources	日益增加的全球资源消费
amplify the consequences	放大了后果
gases emitted in the production of goods	商品生产中排放的气体
significant population growth	人口显著增长
massive consumption levels	超高的消费水平
car-dependent lifestyle	依赖汽车的生活方式
suburban sprawl	(城市)向郊区延伸
reduce the capacity of the planet to absorb CO_2	减弱地球吸收二氧化碳的能力
birth control	生育控制
family size	家庭规模
family planning	计划生育
bigger homes with higher energy demands	房子越大对能源的需求越高
basic energy needs	基础能源需求
consumption patterns	消费模式
ecologically sustainable	生态可持续
risk assessment	风险评估
alternative energy	可替代能源
human activities	人类活动
strike a balance	达到平衡
sustainable development	可持续发展
eliminate tourism plastics	清除旅游塑料(垃圾)
pay a heavy price	付出沉重的代价
remove plastic wrappers	拆掉塑料包装
reduce the size of plastic bags	缩小塑料袋的尺寸
generate solid waste	产生固体废物
cause loss of biodiversity	造成生物多样性的丧失
upgrade drainage systems	升级排水系统
reduce the use of disposable plastics	减少一次性塑料的使用
wooden cutlery and biodegradable cups	木质餐具和可生物降解的杯子

Speaking Activities

Brainstorm

Discuss with your group members the efforts human beings have made to balance economic growth and environmental protection. Then talk about the effectiveness of those measures.

Read and discuss

By 2040, More Than Half of New Cars Will Be Electric

Electric cars make up only a tiny fraction of the automobiles sold worldwide, but that will change quickly, according to an analysis by Bloomberg New Energy Finance.

By 2040, electric cars could make up 57% of all passenger car sales worldwide, the report found. That's up two percentage points from BNEF's 2040 projection last year. Electric vehicles will make up a similar percentage of light commercial vehicle sales in the United States, Europe and China within that time, BNEF predicts.

(Adapted from *cnn. com*)

In China, the government has been trying to promote the use of new energy cars. Electric cars are supposed to reduce the emission of harmful gases produced by internal combustion-powered cars. But even with a lot of government subsidies, the electric cars are still not popularized. Analyze the reasons behind this phenomenon.

Debate

Smoking Worse Than Exhaust

Environmental tobacco smoke is a contributor of air pollution particles. These fine particles are a risk factor for chronic lung disease which can be debilitating and sometimes fatal. They can lead to conditions such as asthma, bronchitis and emphysema, and are also a risk for lung cancer, write the researchers.

(Adapted from *webmd. com*)

Topic for debate: Cigarette smoking in public places should be made illegal.

A3. Extensive Reading

Pros and Cons of 4 Common Alternative Energy Sources

Jeffrey Orloff

There are many reasons why the world is looking for alternative energy sources in an effort to reduce pollutants and greenhouse gases. Alternative or renewable energy sources show significant promise in helping to reduce the number of toxins that are by-products of energy use and help preserve many of the natural resources that we currently use as sources of energy.

To understand how alternative energy use can help preserve the delicate ecological balance of the planet and help us conserve non-renewable energy sources like fossil fuels, it is important to know what type of alternative energy is out there. Let's take a look at some of the most common sources available.

Wind power

Wind energy harnesses the power of the wind to propel the blades of wind turbines. The rotation of turbine blades is converted into electrical current by means of an electrical generator. In the older windmills, wind energy was used to turn mechanical machinery to do physical work, like crushing grain or pumping water. Wind towers are usually built together on wind farms.

Now, electrical currents are harnessed by large-scale wind farms that are used by national electrical grids as well as small individual turbines used for providing electricity to isolated locations or individual homes. In 2005, the worldwide capacity of wind-powered generators was 58,982 megawatts, their production making up less than 1 percent of worldwide electricity use.

Pros. Wind power produces no pollution that can contaminate the environment. Since no chemical processes take place, as in the burning of fossil fuels, there are no harmful by-products left over. Since wind generation is a renewable source of energy, we will never run out of it. Farming and grazing can still take place on land occupied by wind turbines, which can help in the production of biofuels. Wind farms can be built off-shore.

Cons. Wind power is intermittent. Consistent wind is needed for continuous power generation. If wind speed decreases, the turbine lingers and less electricity is generated. Large wind farms can have a negative effect on the scenery.

Solar power

Solar energy is used commonly for heating, cooking, the production of electricity and even in the desalination of seawater. Solar power works by trapping the sun's rays into solar cells where this sunlight is then converted into electricity. Additionally, solar power uses sunlight that hits solar thermal panels to convert sunlight to heat water or air. Other methods include using sunlight that hits parabolic mirrors to heat water (producing steam) or simply opening a room's blinds or window shades to allow entering sunlight to passively heat a room.

Pros. Solar power is a renewable resource. As long as the sun exists, its energy will reach Earth. Solar power generation releases no water or air pollution because there is no chemical reaction from the combustion of fuels. Solar energy can be used very efficiently for practical uses such as heating and lighting. The benefits of solar power are seen frequently to heat pools, spas and water tanks all over the world.

Cons. Solar power does not produce energy if the sun is not shining. Nighttime and cloudy days seriously limit the amount of energy produced. Solar power stations can be very expensive to build.

Geothermal energy

Geothermal literally means"earth heat". Geothermal energy harnesses the heat energy present underneath the earth. Hot rocks under the ground heat water to produce steam. When holes are drilled in the region, the steam that shoots up is purified and is used to drive turbines, which power electric generators.

Pros. If done correctly, geothermal energy produces no harmful by-products. Once a geothermal plant is built, it is generally self-sufficient energy-wise. Geothermal power plants are usually small and have little effect on the natural landscape.

Cons. If done incorrectly, geothermal energy can produce pollutants. Improper drilling into the earth can release hazardous minerals and gases. Geothermal sites are prone to running out of steam.

Hydroelectric energy

Hydroelectric power comes from the potential energy of dammed water driving a water turbine and generator. Another variation is to make use of water's kinetic energy or undammed sources such as tidal power. Hydropower works by harnessing the gravitational descent of a river that is compressed from a long run to a single location with a dam or a flume. This creates a location where concentrated pressure and flow of water can be used to turn turbines or water wheels to drive an electric generator. Electric generators powered by hydropower can be run backward as a motor to pump water back up for later use.

Pros. Water can be accumulated above the dam and released to coincide with peaks in demand. So unlike other types of power stations, hydroelectric power stations can promptly increase to full capacity. Electricity can be generated constantly because there are no outside forces, unlike other forms of alternative energy, which affect the availability of water. Hydroelectric power produces no waste or pollution since there is no chemical reaction to produce power. Water used for hydropower can be reused.

Cons. Dams can be very expensive to build. There needs to be a sufficient and powerful enough supply of water in the area to produce energy.

(Adapted from *thespruce. com*)

Part B Ecological Balance

B1. Introduction

Ecological Balance

Ecology is the science of the study of ecosystems. Ecological balance has been defined by various online dictionaries as "a state of dynamic equilibrium within a community of organisms in which genetic, species and ecosystem diversity remain relatively stable, subject to gradual changes through natural succession" and "a stable balance in the numbers of each species in an ecosystem".

The most important point is that the natural balance in an ecosystem is maintained. This balance may be disturbed due to the introduction of new species, the sudden death of some species, natural hazards or man-made causes. If we disturb any one element, then all the other elements get interrupted in the entire system.

It is usually interpreted that the natural state of any system is the best-preferred state and you should not disturb it. The balance of nature is also considered as the state where the natural communities of plants and animals exist. It is then maintained by competition, adaption and other interactions between the members of a community and their nonliving environment.

History of the theory-balance of nature

The concept that nature maintains its balance has existed for a long time. One of the most proponents of the theory was Herodotus who asserted that there is a perfect relationship between predators and preys which ensures that they remain in steady proportion to one another. In this wonderful relationship predators do not excessively feed on their prey. At some point, the theory of "balance of nature" dominated the ecological research and influenced the management of the natural resources, leading to a popular doctrine among conservationists that nature would thrive if left to take care of itself and human intervention was unacceptable. The balance of nature concept was already in question by the beginning of the 20th century but the concept was abandoned by the scientists in the field of ecology in the last quarter of the century.

Human intervention

The population of predators and prey often exhibit chaotic behaviors within the limit in which the population sizes in ways that may appear random and unpredictable but in real sense obeying the deterministic laws depending on the relationship between the population and the source of food as highlighted by Latke-Volterra equation. Although humans have been accused of destroying the environment, some of their activities have contributed to creating modern day habitats. Some rainforests in Latin America were planted and transplanted by humans. The "fire-stick farming" practiced in Australian Aboriginal is an example of a human activity that modified the ecosystem.

(Adapted from *wwf.panda.org*; *worldatlas.com*)

B2. Passage Reading

B2.1 Nature-led Ecological Problems

The following two passages focus on the role of natural disasters in ecological balance. Read and give your opinions according to the questions. Try to seek diverse perspectives and don't confine yourself to the reference words and expressions given.

Passage One

California Faces Most Dangerous Fire Weather of Year

Guy Kovner

California Fire bought a dozen helicopters for nighttime firefighting as part of a $3.3 billion investment in wildfire response and prevention this year, continuing **a spending spree** that shows no sign of relenting as wildfires of historic proportions **ravage** the state.

The helicopters and 13 new fire engines, along with $165 million in forest health and **fire prevention grants** were among big-ticket items cited in a Legislative Analyst's report on wildfire spending that has **mushroomed** from $800 million 15 years ago.

"We have done more to address wildfires in just the last few years than has been done in all the last few decades," said state Sen. Bill Dodd, D-Napa.

But funding for fire prevention programs appears to have matched only half of the more than $200 million authorized by lawmakers, and Dodd said budget cuts or subtracting money from fire response may be necessary to cover the shortfall.

Meanwhile, a new coalition of business and environmental groups wants California to spend $2 billion next year on wildfire prevention, including a $50 million commitment to prescribed burns, the time-tested protection against wildfires.

"Ecologically we know that California was born and bred of fire and now we're seeing a lot of landscapes destroyed by fire," said Kelly Martin, retired chief of fire and aviation at Yosemite National Park, at a news conference held by the Resilient Forests Coalition. "How we bring fire back into these landscapes is something that is desperately needed."

The coalition's call for fire protection — as opposed to what Martin called "reliance on a suppression industry" — comes as nearly 8,700 wildfires have **scorched** more than 4 million acres, killing 31 people and damaging or destroying more than 9,200 structures this year in California.

Since 2016, **wildland blazes** have blackened more than 8 million acres, more than three times the size of Los Angeles County.

With climate change **exacerbating the threat**, Paul Mason, a vice president at Pacific Forest Trust, said, "We really need to increase the state effort to prepare for fire." The federal government, as the largest forest landowner in California, must also get involved, said David Edelson, forest program director for The Nature Conservancy, noting that more than half of the state's recent wildfires have burned on federal land. "The forests are in crisis, requiring an **all-hands-on-deck** response," Edelson said at the press conference.

(Adapted from *pressdemocrat. com*)

Passage Two

Volcanic Eruption in Philippines Causes Thousands to Flee

Julie McCarthy

A volcano south of the Philippine capital has sent **a massive plume of ash** and steam **spewing** miles into the sky and pushed red-hot **lava** out of its crater, prompting the **evacuation** of thousands of people and the **closure** of Manila's airport.

In a matter of hours on Sunday, the Philippine Institute of Volcanology and Seismology raised the **alert level** for Taal Volcano to Level 4 from Level 1 — with Level 5 being the highest. It warned that a larger **"explosive eruption"** could occur within hours or days.

There were no immediate reports of casualties or major damage from the initial eruption, but authorities advised a total evacuation within a 14-kilometer (8.7-mile) radius of the volcano, which is located about 45 miles south of Manila.

Dozens of earthquakes preceded Sunday's eruption, and authorities warned that a tsunami was possible in the freshwater lake surrounding the volcano. **Flashes of lightning lit up the plume**, lending the scene an otherworldly appearance.

The National Disaster Risk Reduction Management Council, the Philippines' disaster-response agency, said 13,000 villagers were moved away from the area to evacuation centers in Batangas and Cavite provinces. It said nearly 25,000 people had been displaced by the eruption.

Some residents refused to leave their homes and farms, officials said, while others reportedly could not leave because of a lack of transportation or **poor visibility** from the thick ash, the AP says.

"Our people are **panicking** due to the volcano because they want to save their livelihood, their pigs and herds of cows," Mayor Wilson Maralit of Balete town told local DZMM radio, according to the news agency. "We're trying to stop them from returning and warning that the volcano can explode again anytime and hit them."

The Volcanology Institute cautioned that **fine ashfall** could cause breathing problems, especially among young children and the elderly, and advised the public in affected areas to use face masks or wet towels to protect themselves. It also advised motorists that the ash could reduce visibility and make roads slippery.

In Manila, long lines formed at shops selling face masks, with many residents no doubt remembering the 1991 eruption of Mount Pinatubo, about 55 miles northwest of the capital, an eruption that killed more than 350 people and **blanketed the area** for miles around in thick ash.

Ash clouds stretched 62 miles north, forcing authorities to shut down Ninoy Aquino International Airport and causing the cancellation of more than 500 international and domestic flights, according to the Associated Press. The Civil Aviation Authority of the Philippines said it would also shut down an airfield at Clark Freeport Zone, home of the former U. S. air base, if ash **threatened flights** there.

President Rodrigo Duterte's office ordered a halt to government work in Manila and the closure of all schools in the capital. It advised private companies to do the same.

The area immediately around Taal has been designated a "**permanent danger zone**". It last erupted in 1977, and another eruption in 1911 killed an estimated 1,500 people.

(Adapted from *npr. org*)

Opinion sharing

(a) How many natural disasters do you know?
(b) Describe a natural disaster you have witnessed, experienced or heard of. Talk about its impacts.
(c) It is said that natural disasters like wildfire are a self-healing process of nature. Comment on the viewpoint and share your opinions.
(d) Do you think human activities have anything to do with natural disasters? Why?

Reference Words and Expressions

arson	纵火
devastating	毁灭性的

lightening	闪电
self-healing	自愈
flammable	易燃的
evacuate	撤离
earthquake	地震

fire season	火灾易发季节
seasonal wind	季风
faulty electrical equipment	电气设备故障
burn at a shocking speed	以惊人的速度燃烧
scorch the land	烧焦土地
occur on their own	自发产生
human causes	人为原因
unattended camp fire	无人看管的营火
debris fire	残火
discarded cigarette	丢弃的烟头
downed powerline	落地的电线
play an integral role in nature	在自然界中扮演不可或缺的角色
burn the dead and decaying matter	燃烧死的和腐烂的东西
return nutrients to the soil	把养分还给土壤
remove harmful insects from an ecosystem	从生态系统中清除害虫
remove disease-ridden plants	清除病株
thin forest canopies and undergrowth	使树冠和灌木丛变稀疏
allow sunlight to reach the forest floor	让阳光照射到森林地面
allow a new generation of seedlings to grow	让新一代的幼苗得以生长
volcanic eruption	火山喷发
explosive force	爆炸力
lava river	熔岩河
viscous magma	黏性岩浆
molten rocks	融化的岩石
pose dangers	造成危险
pyroclastic flow	火山碎屑流
hot rocks, ash and toxic gas	热岩、灰和有毒气体
bury cities and towns	埋葬城镇
create fertile soil	生成肥沃的土地
craft landscape	打造陆地景观
allow civilization to flourish	让文明蓬勃发展
warning signs	警告标志

immediate danger	直接的危险
rock the ground	让大地摇晃
tremendously destructive	极具破坏性
collapsing buildings	倒塌的楼房
emergency planning	应急预案
compounded by mud slides, fires, floods	再加上泥石流、火灾、洪水
buildings that sway rather than break	只摇晃不倒塌的建筑
under the stress of earthquakes	在地震压力下

Speaking Activities

Discussion

To a certain extent, a pandemic could be viewed as a natural disaster. In the face of a pandemic, some countries adopt the strategy of "herd immunity" — survival of the fittest. Do you think it is reasonable? Give reasons.

Debate

In the face of natural disasters, mankind is usually weak and helpless. From our perspective, natural disasters do more damage than good. But people are making efforts to minimize the harmful effects of natural disasters and harness some forces of nature.

Topic for debate: Which is more powerful, man or nature?

Interview: Disaster relief

Flooding in urban areas can be caused by flash floods, coastal floods or river floods, but there is also a specific flood type that is called urban flooding. Urban flooding is specific in the fact that the cause is a lack of drainage in an urban area.

Scenario: A heavy rain caused severe flooding in a big city. Now the local news agency is going to interview people involved in this disaster:

local government officials
first responders
the affected residents
witnesses

Work in groups. One of you is the interviewer, others role play the above listed interviewees. Your questions can cover the following points:

(a) What do you think is the cause of the flooding?
(b) How does the flooding affect your life?
(c) How are we to cope?

(d) After the interview, the interviewer summarizes the ideas of the interviewees.

B2.2 Human-made Ecological Damage

The following two passages focus on the human activities that affect the ecological balance. Read and give your opinions according to the questions. Try to seek diverse perspectives and don't confine yourself to the reference words and expressions given.

Passage One

By Killing Whales, Is Japan Trying to Revive a Dying Industry?

Ivan Watson

For the whale hunters, the inaugural expedition was a big success.

Hours after heading out to sea, their ships returned with the **carcasses** of two freshly **harpooned** minke whales, their huge, gaping maws draped off the sterns of the vessels.

At a ceremony before the fleet went out on July 1, Yoshifumi Kai, chairman of the Japan Small-Type Whaling Association, had given an emotional speech to an assembly of whalers, law-makers and the mayor of the northern Japanese port city of Kushiro.

"I'm so moved my heart is shaking," he said.

This was an important day. Japan was **lifting a 30-year ban** on **commercial whaling** in its waters.

In 1986, the International Whaling Commission (IWC) announced a worldwide moratorium on commercial whaling. In late 2018, however, Japan decided to withdraw from the IWC — a move welcomed by its whale industry but **condemned** by **environmental campaigners** who believed it would threaten endangered species of whale.

But with Japan's appetite for whale meat in decline, why is the country so **committed** to killing whales?

The septuagenarian Maeda brothers have decades of experience in pursuing whales.

"Finding whales is a part of my life," the elder Maeda said, as he steered his boat towards a minke whale to give the half a dozen Japanese tourists on board a closer look.

When asked about the **resumption** of commercial whaling, none of the tourists objected.

"Of course, it should restart," the elder Maeda said. "Japan has a **culinary culture** of whales."

Maeda has no plans to revive his former career, however. He enjoys showing tourists fin whales, the second largest of the world's whale species.

"I will continue to lead cruises, and the whale hunters can catch the whales," he said. "I want both to **co-exist**."

Tokyo has defended its right to hunt whales, arguing it is a **vital part** of Japanese culture and **maritime tradition.**

"Japan is an island nation surrounded by the ocean and we have been using the whale as food since ancient times," says Kiyoshi Ejima, a lawmaker from Japan's ruling Liberal Democrat Party and a staunch supporter of the whaling industry.

Critics argue that it's a dying industry that is kept alive only by government subsidies. Japan's Fisheries Agency has allocated the equivalent of about $463 million to supporting whaling for the 2019 fiscal year.

"If whaling is forced to **sink or swim**, this industry will drown very quickly," said Ramage, from the International Fund for Animal Welfare.

Still, restaurants in Tokyo decorate their entrances with paintings of whales at sea and proudly celebrate the culinary tradition of serving this **niche meat**.

Now that Japan has withdrawn from the IWC, whalers will no longer hunt in international waters but will pursue them in an economic exclusion zone, which extends 200 nautical miles from the Japanese coast.

(Adapted from *cnn.com*)

Passage Two

Arctic Oil Drilling

As if the impacts of climate change weren't enough, big fossil fuel companies have now set their sites on **exploiting** the oil that lies deep in Arctic waters.

The people and animals that live in the Arctic depend on its **unique ecosystem** to survive. Yet major companies like Shell and Exxon are making aggressive moves to **usher** in a new "oil rush" in the Arctic Ocean. In some places it has already begun. Russian oil giant Gazprom has already begun producing small amounts oil from the Arctic in the ocean north of Russia.

Here's why we can't let ANY drilling in the Arctic continue.

The long history of oil spills around the world has made one thing clear: the only way to prevent an oil spill is to keep oil in the ground.

Fragile Arctic ice and **tricky weather conditions** make a spill in the region even more likely. In a review of Shell's plans to drill in the Alaskan Arctic Ocean, the U. S. Department of the Interior found that there's a 75 percent chance of a major oil spill if an oil company finds oil and produces it. Even though the U. S. Department of Interior is taking the Arctic off the table for oil drilling for the next two years, it's critically important that the region is closed to ALL new oil drilling forever.

No oil company has ever successfully **cleaned up a major spill.**

In 1989, the Exxon Valdez spilled 11 million gallons of oil into Alaska's Prince William Sound. Exxon spent $2 billion trying to clean up and recovered less than 7 percent of the oil spilled.

In 2010, the BP Deepwater Horizon blowout spilled up to 200 million barrels into the Gulf of Mexico. Of that, only about 8 percent was **recovered** or **burned off.**

Extreme conditions — including icy waves that reach 50 feet — make response in the event of an Arctic spill even more difficult. The nearest response stations to Arctic drilling sites are located thousands of miles away.

For the sake of the people and animals that call the Arctic home — not to mention the global climate — we must keep offshore oil in the ground **for good**. There's no climate-safe future that involves drilling in the Arctic Ocean.

It's the only way to prevent a devastating spill and end our dependence on fossil fuels.

(Adapted from *greenpeace.org*)

Opinion sharing

(a) Similar to the whale-eating culture, Chinese people also eat bird's nest and shark's fin. How can we cope with traditional eating culture and eco-balance?

(b) Why are gas cars still more widely used than electric cars if we are promoting renewable energy?

(c) Can you make a list of dilemmas when your personal convenience contradicts with environmental protection?

(d) Does online shopping protect or destroy the environment?

(e) What can you do to reduce the use of paper? Give examples.

Reference Words and Expressions

threat	威胁
menace	威胁(语气强于 threat)
carpooling	拼车
marine ecosystem	海洋生态系统
combat climate change	应对气候变化
sustain fish stocks	维持鱼类资源
provide nutrients to phytoplankton	为浮游植物提供营养
whale poop fertilizes microscopic plants	鲸鱼粪便给微小植物施肥

absorb carbon from the atmosphere	吸收大气中的碳
ocean's gardeners	海洋的园丁
animal population	动物种群
conservation of species	物种保护
oil and gas extraction	石油和天然气开采
disrupt wildlife habitat	破坏野生动物栖息地
human movement and vehicle traffic	人类活动和车辆交通活动
damage animals' nesting or breeding grounds	破坏动物的巢穴或繁殖地
harm fish and marine mammals	危害鱼类和海洋哺乳动物
preserve the beauty of the land	保护这片土地的美丽
fragile ecosystem	脆弱的生态系统
oil spills can be deadly to animals	石油泄漏对动物是致命的
dangerous chemicals	危险的化学物质
long-term environmental impacts	长期环境影响
devastating effects	毁灭性影响
protect our planet	保护我们的星球
conserve natural resources	保护自然资源
finite resources	有限的资源
promote sustainable development	促进可持续发展
overexploit fish	过度捕捞鱼类
protect at-risk fish populations	保护濒危鱼类种群
stop buying endangered or protected animals	停止购买濒危或者受保护的动物
avoid single-use plastics	避免使用一次性塑料用品
substitute with durable items	用耐用物品替代
use a more fuel-efficient car	使用更省油的车
take public transportation	乘坐公共交通工具
improve recycling systems	改善回收系统
sustainable agriculture practices	可持续农业实践
keep soil healthy	保持土壤健康
use fewer chemicals	少用化学品
biological pest control	生物害虫防治
natural fertilizers	天然肥料
optimize resource use	优化资源利用
mimic the natural destruction	模仿自然破坏
regeneration patterns of nature	自然的再生模式
treat waste water before discharging it	排放前处理废水
maintaining plant and animal biodiversity	维护动植物多样性
encourage the public to conserve resources	鼓励公众节约资源

educate people about the importance	教育人们认识到重要性
individual contributions	个人贡献
preserve and restore the natural environment	保护和恢复自然环境
get involved in conservation efforts	参与保护工作

Speaking Activities

Debate

Nowadays, many people are starting to use e-books instead of paper books. E-book reduces the use of paper and is thus environmental-friendly, but paper book is more physically comfortable.

Topic for debate: E-books will replace paper books.

Presentation

Human-beings not only feed on many animals but also kill animals for their body parts. Fur clothing is a necessity for people living in extremely cold places and also forms an important part of fashion. To protect animal rights, faux fur is replacing real fur in the clothing industry. But faux fur is adding plastic waste to our planet.
Work in groups and discuss the following aspects:
—The benefits and downsides of fur clothing;
—The benefits and downsides of faux fur;
—Is faux fur a better replacement of real fur? Give reasons.

Discussion

Think of five modern products that are indispensable in our life but also unfriendly to the environment. If you have to choose among them, which one can you live without? Then, put them in order of their importance in your life. Give reasons.

B3. Extensive Reading

8 Animals that Recycle in Their Everyday Lives

Bryan Nelson

Most animals live in a delicate ecological balance with their natural surroundings. It's simply the most efficient formula for survival: take only what is needed, and waste as little of it as possible. But a few animals take "reduce, reuse and recycle" to the next level.

Here are eight animals that are some of nature's best recyclers.

Birds

Perhaps nature's greatest recyclers are birds. Many urban species have adapted to life in human environments by building their nests with whatever is available, which often includes anything from discarded string and newspapers to paper clips and plastic.

Bowerbirds from New Guinea and Australia, which construct elaborate and garish "bowers" in order to attract mates, will often collect colorful trash (such as bottle caps and plastics) and repurpose it for bower decoration.

Of course, birds like pigeons and gulls also take advantage of food waste that is left behind by humans, gobbling up what they can.

Hermit crabs

Hermit crabs don't grow their own shells, so to protect themselves they have to salvage shells abandoned by other sea life, usually from sea snails. But they'll actually use whatever they can find, which often includes glass bottles and cans. People who keep hermit crabs as pets also have the option of providing them with artificial shells, which can be made from recycled materials.

As a crab grows, it must often seek out new shells that provide a better fit. Hermit crabs also may eat their old shells for nutrients. In this way, these cute crustaceans are constantly recycling dwellings that would otherwise go to waste.

Orb-weaver spiders

All spiderwebs represent remarkable engineering feats, but few match the eco-friendly design showcased by some orb-weaver spiders. Particularly the species *Cyclosa ginnaga*, which decorates its web with whatever debris it can find, such as leaves and twigs. Though the ultimate purpose of the decoration is for luring prey or for concealing the web, this spider's use of readily available materials is still worth noting.

Many orb-weaver spiders rebuild their nests every day, so they are always busy recycling. This helps keep both their webs and their surrounding environment clean.

Dung beatles

To the dung beetle, even poop is a valuable resource. This insect lives to collect and repurpose your poop. Not only do dung beetles build their homes out of feces, but they also eat it and lay their eggs in it. Adult male dung beetles are sometimes referred to as "rollers", since their waste-collection strategy is to roll excrement into balls and offer it to a female, so they can easily roll it away together.

The environmental value of dung beetles shouldn't be understated. It's estimated that dung beetles save the United States cattle industry $380 million annually by repurposing livestock feces.

Octopuses

Octopuses are probably the smartest invertebrates on the planet, and nothing quite displays their cunning as much as their tool use. Several species, such as the coconut octopus, have been observed building shelters out of discarded debris. These makeshift homes are built from anything found lying around, from cracked coconut shells, to abandoned sea shells, to glass jars and other containers thrown away as trash. It just goes to show that one creature's waste is another creature's treasure.

Corals

It has been estimated that 75 percent of all coral reefs around the world are threatened, but there is also reason to hope. Though sensitive to variations in their environment, these animals are also remarkably adaptable in that they are able to attach themselves to just about any hard surface they can find. This includes shipwrecks, undersea pipelines, and even oil rigs. By repurposing wreckage on the seafloor, they also provide habitat for the countless other species that rely on the ecology of coral reefs for sustenance.

Butterflies

A creature that really knows how to reuse is the monarch butterfly. Before making their transformation into elegant butterflies, monarch caterpillars eat their old home. The monarch lays its eggs and the larva begins to grow inside the egg. When its time in the egg is finished, the larva chews its way to freedom, and eats the rest of its egg home.

Lobsters

Lobsters, which grow by molting, have found a way of making use of their old shells. These ocean dwellers grow significantly during their lifetime. When a lobster molts, it first absorbs the minerals that caused its shell to harden, softening the shell, and allowing itself to break free. During their wait for a new shell to form, lobsters, which are scavengers by nature, sometimes eat their own nutrition-rich molted shell.

(Adapted from *treehugger. com*)

References

What Is Pollution? *Britannica*. Retrieved from https://www. britannica. com/science/pollution-environment on March 20th, 2021.

Types of Pollution. *BYJU'S*. Retrieved from https://byjus. com/biology/types-of-pollution/ on March 20th, 2021.

Kacey Deamer. (2016). Scientists Determine Cause of London's 1952 "Killer Fog". *CBS News*. Retrieved from https://www. cbsnews. com/news/londons-1952-killer-fog-cause-revealed/ on March 20th, 2021.

(2017). The Clean Air Act. *Friends of the Earth*. Retrieved from https://friendsoftheearth.uk/climate/london-smog-and-1956-clean-air-act on March 20th, 2021.

Nishan Degnarain. (2020). Japan to Release Radioactive Fukushima Water into Ocean. *Forbes*. Retrieved from https://www.forbes.com/sites/nishandegnarain/2020/10/18/japan-to-release-radioactive-fukishima-water-into-ocean/#4125718b4329 on March 20th, 2021.

Fireworks Ban. *Travel China Guide*. Retrieved from https://www.travelchinaguide.com/essential/holidays/new-year/firework.htm on March 19th, 2021.

Katrin Büchenbacher. (2019). Garbage Sorting. *CGTN*. Retrieved from https://news.cgtn.com/news/2019-08-13/Is-garbage-sorting-the-new-normal-in-China-J7yu1UDsSk/index.html on March 20th, 2021.

Jordyn Cormier. (2016). Which Is Worse for the Planet: Beef or Cars? *EcoWatch*. Retrieved from https://www.ecowatch.com/which-is-worse-for-the-planet-beef-or-cars-1919932136.html on March 20th, 2021.

Oishimaya Sen Nag. (2018). Environmental Impacts of Tourism. *World Atlas*. Retrieved from https://www.worldatlas.com/articles/what-are-the-negative-effects-of-tourism-on-the-environment.html on March 20th, 2021.

Peter Valdes-Dapean. (2019). By 2040, More Than Half of New Cars will Be Electric. *CNN BUSINESS*. Retrieved from https://edition.cnn.com/2019/05/15/business/electric-car-outlook-bloomberg/index.html on March 20th, 2021.

Miranda Hitti. (2004). Smoking Worse Than Exhaust for Air Pollution. *WebMD*. Retrieved from https://www.webmd.com/lung/news/20040823/smoking-worse-than-exhaust-for-air-pollution on March 20th, 2021.

Jeffrey Orloff. (2019). Pros and Cons of 4 Common Alternative Energy Sources. *The Spruce*. Retrieved from https://www.thespruce.com/the-most-common-alternative-energy-sources-2941105 on March 20th, 2021.

Ecological Balance. *WWF-Panda*. Retrieved from https://wwf.panda.org/discover/knowledge_hub/teacher_resources/webfieldtrips/ecological_balance/ on March 19th, 2021.

John Misachi. (2018). Ecological Balance. *World Atlas*. Retrieved from https://www.worldatlas.com/articles/what-is-the-balance-of-nature.html on March 20th, 2021.

Guy Kovner. (2020). California Faces Most Dangerous Fire Weather of Year. *The Press Democrat*. Retrieved from https://www.pressdemocrat.com/article/news/wildfire-spending-escalates-as-blazes-ravage-california/ on March 20th, 2021.

Julie McCarthy. (2020). Volcanic Eruption in Philippines Causes Thousands to Flee. *NPR*. Retrieved from https://www.npr.org/2020/01/13/795815351/volcanic-eruption-in-philippines-causes-thousands-to-flee on March 20th, 2021.

Ivan Watson. (2019). By Killing Whales, Is Japan Trying to Revive a Dying Industry? *CNN*. Retrieved from https://edition. cnn. com/2019/07/02/asia/japan-resumes-whaling-hnk-intl/index. html on March 20th, 2021.

Arctic Oil Drilling. *Green Peace*. Retrieved from https://www. greenpeace. org/usa/arctic/issues/oil-drilling/ on March 20th, 2021.

Bryan Nelson. (2020). 8 Animals that Recycle in Their Everyday Lives. *TreeHugger*. Retrieved from https://www. treehugger. com/animals-that-recycle-in-their-everyday-lives-4869312 on March 20th, 2021.

Unit 5 Human

Part A Personality and Quotient

A1. Introduction

Personality Types

Usually, people classify the personalities of different people on the basis of their physique, nature and appearance. But how they behave generally is also one inevitable aspect that defines people's personalities. Some of us may be highly outgoing and outspoken, making friends with people we meet easily. On the other hand, some others may be reserved enough to concentrate their energies more towards themselves than on those around them. While the former group is categorized as extroverts, the latter is termed as introverts.

Yes, some of us feel invigorated in the presence of other people. Yet, others simply enjoy being alone. They do not need anyone to enjoy life and develop as a person.

Introvert personality

An introvert personality is what makes a person keep his thoughts and feelings to himself. Introversion does not often let a person seek inspiration or contentment from an outside source. For that matter, the person is enough in himself. He is his own friend.

Of course, introverts get into touch with people and make friends too. But rarely do they get close to anyone. They like to share their views with one or two very close people. They keep their love for a few selected people and can't handle parties or a group of people. In most cases, these people create a line which no one can cross. Or else, they prefer sitting quietly and listening while meeting a group. They often come up with one line in between, which is notable. And it never means that they are getting bored. They love to sit in silence when amid too many people.

Extrovert personality

Extroverts are the people-friendly people. Remaining with their friends and / or those they are familiar with makes them feel utterly comfortable and content. They may feel bored when alone, and they enjoy themselves best when amid a group. Being around people, in fact, makes them energetic and spirited.

The trait of extroversion in a person can make him the center of attraction at any party. The reason is simple. He is light-hearted, humorous and, above all, outspoken. He can be friends with anyone in a matter of seconds. Extroverts dare to do anything that could bring attention to them.

Differences between introverts and extroverts

Although introvert and extrovert personality types differ from one another on various grounds, the major difference between the two is their source of rejuvenation. While for extroverts, this may mean interaction or excursions with friends and family, the same may mean reading a book or listening to music for introverts.

Introverts are often misunderstood by extrovert personalities, and vice-versa. Introverts are extremely good listeners, but still like to spend most of their time alone. Extroverts tend to believe that these people are shy, depressed and boring. On the contrary, introverts believe that extroverts hardly care about anyone's feelings and only think about enjoying themselves and partying. Both may be right in their own way, and may still not understand the other fully. But, an introvert and an extrovert, if they understand each other, may make the best couple.

Comparison between Introvert and Extrovert

Introvert	Extrovert
Involved more with themselves.	Involved more with friends and family.
Get energized when alone.	Get bored when alone.
Have a few friends.	Have a lot of friends.
Sit quietly and listen.	Speak a lot and usually remain in limelight.

Types of Quotients

Emotional quotient

"Your EQ is the level of your ability to understand other people, what motivates them and how to work cooperatively with them," says Howard Gardner, the influential

Harvard theorist. Five major categories of emotional intelligence skills are recognized by researchers in this area.

Understanding the Five Categories of Emotional Intelligence.

Self-awareness. The ability to recognize an emotion as it "happens" is the key to your EQ. Developing self-awareness requires tuning in to your true feelings. If you evaluate your emotions, you can manage them.

Self-regulation. You often have little control over when you experience emotions. You can, however, have some say in how long an emotion will last by using a number of techniques to alleviate negative emotions such as anger, anxiety or depression. A few of these techniques include recasting a situation in a more positive light, taking a long walk and meditation or prayer.

Motivation. To motivate yourself for any achievement requires clear goals and a positive attitude. Although you may have a predisposition to either a positive or a negative attitude, you can with effort practice learn to think more positively. If you catch negative thoughts as they occur, you can reframe them in more positive terms — which will help you achieve your goals.

Empathy. The ability to recognize how people feel is important to success in your life and career. The more skillful you are at discerning the feelings behind others' signals, the better you can control the signals you send them.

Social skills. The development of good interpersonal skills is tantamount to success in your life and career. In today's always-connected world, everyone has immediate access to technical knowledge. Thus, "people skills" are even more important now because you must possess a high EQ to better understand, empathize and negotiate with others in a global economy.

Intelligence quotient

In science, the term intelligence typically refers to what we could call academic or cognitive intelligence. In their book on intelligence, professors Resing and Drenth answered the question "What is intelligence?" using the following definition, "The whole of cognitive or intellectual abilities required to obtain knowledge, and to use that knowledge in a good way to solve problems that have a well-described goal and structure."

In ordinary language, one could say that intelligence refers to how smart or clever you are.

The first intelligence tests used in the field of psychology

The scales designed by Binet and Simon were the first intelligent tests that became widely accepted at the beginning of the 20th century. The Alpha and Beta army tests, that were used in World War I to assess military personnel, became very popular.

In recent years, the Wechsler scales are the most widely used instruments in the field of psychology for measuring intelligence. The designer of these tests, Wechsler, published his first scale in the 1930s. He used material from the Binet and Alpha and Beta tests to make his test. An important feature of his test was that when calculating the IQ, this test took age into account. In other words, in the computation of the IQ, an age-correction takes place. Because of this feature, the IQ stays constant over the life span.

IQ is an acronym for Intelligence Quotient. The IQ is a measurement of your intelligence and is expressed in a number.

A person's IQ can be calculated by having the person take an intelligence test. The average IQ is 100. If you achieve a score higher than 100, you are smarter than the average person, and a lower score means you are (somewhat) less smart.

An IQ tells you what your score is on a particular intelligence test, often compared to your age-group. The test has a mean score of 100 points and a standard deviation of 15 points. What does this standard deviation mean? It means that 68 percent of the population score an IQ within the interval 85-115. And that 95 percent of the population scores within the interval 70-130.

(Adapted from *theydiffer. com*; *psychcentral. com*; *123test. com*)

A2. Passage Reading

A2. 1 Extroversion and Introversion

The following two passages focus on current perspectives on personality. Read and give your opinions according to the questions. Try to seek diverse perspectives and don't confine yourself to the reference words and expressions given.

Passage One

Do Extroverts Make Better Leaders?

Sally Percy

There is a general perception that you're better off in the workplace — and in life — if you're an extrovert. Understandably, this perception tends to **be vociferously propagated** by extroverts themselves, who tend to be "loud and proud". But what does the research suggest?

In *What Could Be Bad News for Introverts*, a new study by the University of Toronto Scarborough has found that extroverts do **have an edge** that **boosts their chances of** success. The study reviewed existing scientific literature relating to extroversion in the workplace from multiple countries. It found that extroverts enjoy a distinct advantage in four categories: emotional, interpersonal, motivational and performance-related.

"These four appear to really **capture the strongest positive effects** of extroversion at work," says Michael Wilmot, the academic who led the study. Wilmot argues that extroversion is linked with **a greater motivation** to achieve positive goals — for example, a desired reward through work. It is also closely associated with experiencing positive emotions more regularly.

As happy employees are usually more satisfied, they tend to work harder and **are** perceived to be better leaders as a result. Extroverts' **positive demeanor** also helps to **buffer them from stress** or **adverse experiences** at work.

Since extroverts enjoy the company of others, they tend to adapt better to different social situations and **are adept at persuasion**, which is a strong leadership skill. The high performance of extroverts tends to come about as a result of the combination of the three other advantages.

"If you're motivated to achieve a goal at work, if you're feeling positive, and if you're good at dealing with people, you're probably going to perform better on the job," says Wilmot. "These advantages appear to have **a cumulative effect** over the span of one's career."

While the research suggests that extroverts have plenty to be positive about — even more positive than they usually are — Wilmot says introverts should not be discouraged. They are not at an inevitable disadvantage.

First, Wilmot points out that few people can be defined purely as an introvert or extrovert since everyone **displays a range of extroverted and introverted behaviors.** Secondly, numerous other characteristics contribute to workplace success, including **cognitive ability**, conscientiousness and the ability to regulate negative emotions. There are also many jobs, such as computer programming, where having introverted characteristics such as listening skills or the ability to focus, would be more beneficial than more extroverted characteristics such as sociability.

(Adapted from *forbes. com*)

Passage Two

Bias Against Introverts

Kathy Caprino

This month, something truly upsetting happened to one of my children. When that happens, as a mother, I get very serious about understanding the roots of the troubling incident, then doing my best to support my child effectively through it. In this case, I believe that what happened isn't an isolated incident at all, but a culturally-supported one that affects millions of people today.

My son, who is an introvert and is somewhat shy (introversion and shyness are not the same), experienced what I believe is **out-and-out** bias against introversion. He's in college studying Business and Finance, and in one class, the **mandate** (in order to get a good grade) was that every student participate fully every single class by speaking up, contributing ideas and actively adding to the class discussion. The written mandate indicated that just attending the class each day and actively listening (without speaking and contributing) would grant no higher than a "D" in the "participation" segment of the overall grade.

Here's the problem, from my view, with this mandate: For my son, and millions of other introverts (it is estimated that introverts represent 26-50% of the population), speaking up in a class environment on a continual basis, having to brainstorm each class **on the spot** and arrive at — and share publicly — new ideas without having time to think them through and raising his hand to lead a group discussion are all activities that are very deep challenges. These are in direct opposition to his preferred and natural style of operating. For extroverts, on the other hand, this type of public speaking, on-demand brainstorming, and group participation are much more comfortable and easier. Forcing each student to perform in the exact same way in order to get a good grade **smacks** to me of bias.

In 2013, Susan Cain, a Harvard law school graduate and former attorney and negotiator, burst **on the scene** with her bestselling book *Quiet: The Power of Introverts in a World that Can't Stop Talking*. She explained that she had previously viewed her quiet, reserved nature as a disadvantage, something to be overcome. In fact, she experienced **shame and humiliation** at being introverted. But as she began researching introversion as **a personality trait**, she learned that what many people perceive as a weakness is in reality a strength — one that most Americans (including business managers, leaders, teachers, etc.) fail to appreciate. Cain defines introversion as the preference for quieter, more minimally stimulating environments, where extroverts feel at their best and crave a high degree of stimulation. For introverts, the optimal zone is much lower. Her TED talk — *The Power of Introverts* (with 18.3 million views) — is riveting.

In the past few years, I began to see and understand my son's introversion for what it was, rather than "shyness" or a stubborn **reluctance** to share his ideas or speak in public with others he just met. I also began focusing more intently on my own biases against introversion, and saw that they were **rampant**. While I used to see staff members or colleagues as "not able to **think on their feet**," or "so quiet that it hurts them," I now see the keen power of minds, their intense creativity and brilliant ideas, along with their ability to comfortably share power with others rather than needing to put their mark on other people's ideas.

In my son's situation, do I think it was wrong of this professor to demand full, active participation in every class (meaning, requiring the students to speak up each time with new ideas and to lead out loud strongly in each class discussion) as a criterion for getting a good grade?

(Adapted from *forbes.com*)

Opinion sharing

(a) Can introverts and extroverts be friends?
(b) What misconceptions do people make about introverts?
(c) Do you know about ambiverts? Under what circumstances can an introvert become an extrovert, or vice versa?
(d) According to different traits of introverts and extroverts, what kind of jobs do you think suit them respectively? Give your reasons.
(e) When pursuing someone, which one do you think has more advantages, introverts or extroverts? Why?

Reference Words and Expressions

ambivert	具有中间性格的人
extroversion	外向性(性格)
introversion	内向性(性格)
wallflower	不善社交的人(多指女孩)
social-loving	爱社交的
weirdo	怪人
emotional awareness	情绪觉察
drama queen	小题大做的人
party animal	热衷于参加聚会的人
biologically based behavioral patterns	基于生物学的行为模式
an internal focus	内在聚焦
feel comfortable in the spotlight	在聚光灯下感觉舒适
be engrossed by reflection	全神贯注于思考
social interactions	社会交往

persistent contemplation	长时间的沉思
be engaged in social circles	参与社交圈
verbal interaction	言语交流
calm considerations	冷静考虑
mindful introspection	深思熟虑
feel energized from collective activities	在集体活动中感到精力充沛
flourish when retreating into themselves	回到自己的世界里会变得强大
need a large circle of acquaintances to excel	熟人众多的情况下会出类拔萃
prefer a small but cohesive network	喜欢一个小却有凝聚力的人际网络
share one's thoughts and opinions glibly	畅所欲言
hold one's views and ideas closer to their heart	使自己的观点和想法更贴近内心
ruminate on the ideas prior to revealing them	在表达想法前先反省
inner strength	内在力量
face personal crises	面对个人危机
be inclined to avoid conflicts	倾向于避免冲突
be keen on listening intently	专心倾听
formulate opinions thoughtfully	深思熟虑地提出意见
talk things through	把事情说清楚
meet new friends and share personal info	结识新朋友，分享个人信息
be intrusive	侵扰
alone time	独处时光
social engagement	社会参与
be able to speak fluidly out loud	能流利地大声说话
thrive as independent thinkers	作为独立思考者很强大
exhibit positivity or optimism	表现得积极或乐观
encourage collaboration	鼓励合作

Speaking Activities

Brainstorm

Think of some examples of successful people. As far as you are concerned, are they introverts or extroverts? Do you agree that personality is crucial for success?

Read and discuss

Nowadays many employers use personality tests to help find a candidate whose character traits are best suited and a good fit for a specific position. A pre-employment assessment test is designed to reveal particular aspects of a candidate's personality and estimate the likelihood that they will excel in such a position.

Now chances are that college graduates take personality tests (e. g., The Big Five Personality Test) to find out more about who they are and their strengths before choosing a career. Besides, they are also given such tests when hunting jobs. Sometimes if test-takers screw up, they cannot proceed to do the job interviews.

What do you think of the significance of personality tests in job interviews?

Read and discuss

Personality is different from character as shown in the chart below:

Personality vs. Character

Basis of Comparison	Personality	Character
Meaning	Personality refers to the range of distinctive personal qualities and traits of an individual.	A character refers to a set of morals and beliefs that defines how we treat or behave with others and ourselves.
Represents	Who we seem to be?	Who we actually are?
Traits	Personal and physical.	Mental and moral.
Nature	Subjective.	Objective.
Expression	Outer appearance and behavior of a person.	Traits of a person that are abstract.
Change	May change over time.	Remains same.

From the chart, we know that personality may change over time and it is subject to diverse situations. For example, your outer appearance and behavior may be different when you are at home facing your parents and when you hang out with friends. Think about how your personality change on different occasions and share with your classmates.

(Adapted from *keydifferences.com*)

A2.2 EQ and IQ

The following two passages focus on EQ and IQ. Read and give your opinions according to the questions. Try to seek diverse perspectives and don't confine yourself to the reference words and expressions given.

Passage One

Engage Emotional Intelligence to Better Your Relationships

Stephanie Burns

Emotional intelligence is increasingly becoming a mainstream importance in relationships. Defined by helpguide. org as the "ability to understand, use and manage your own emotions in positive ways to **relieve stress**, communicate effectively, **empathize with others**, overcome challenges and **defuse conflict**," emotional intelligence centers in reading emotions in guiding your relationships with others.

This is particularly important in your business: with team members, employees, clients, and in networking. Emotional intelligence not only has the capacity to better relationships, but expand your own influence over those you have relationships with. Here are three ways to engage emotional intelligence to better your relationships and **expand your influence.**

Firstly, recognize that everyone perceives the world from the perspective of their own emotions and motivations. In order to "win" in their perspective of the world and be as effective as possible, begin to ask questions and be observational in your meetings and calls. Just as you ask a potential client a host of questions to determine their motivations and emotions on an onboarding call, **exercise the same level of interest** in all of your relationships. Another way to think about this is through empathy: understanding the other's pain should be similar to taking their pain on as your own.

Secondly, see the value in what others contribute. Ultimately, everyone wants to feel that they are valued in their relationships. If they don't feel this way, they're less likely to invest more time and energy into the relationship. Influence is not about helping others see your value and what you contribute, it's about helping others see their own value in what they contribute. In most situations, people naturally **hold back** when they feel they have nothing to offer. As you help others understand their importance in a relationship or to a team, they will revere you more as a leader because you revered them first.

Finally, **another pillar of emotional intelligence** is the ability to recognize your own emotions and how they may have an effect on others. Take the time to check in with yourself can spell the difference between **distancing yourself from** your relationships or keeping them close. Do a **mental and emotional check-in** every morning, and midday if something has been particularly stressful. The key is to not **stuff it down** — you can feel the emotions, but make sure you're expressing them in a healthy manner.

Ultimately, emotional intelligence will not only strengthen your interpersonal relationships, but it will help you become more self-aware which can only benefit you in the long run.

(Adapted from *forbes. com*)

Passage Two

How Much Does IQ Matter?

Alison Pearce Stevens

IQ, short for intelligence quotient, is a measure of a person's **reasoning ability**. In short, it is supposed to **gauge** how well someone can use information and logic to answer questions or make predictions. IQ tests begin to assess this by measuring short- and long-term memory. They also measure how well people can **solve puzzles** and **recall information** they've heard — and how quickly.

Every student can learn, no matter how intelligent. But some students struggle in school because of a weakness in one specific area of intelligence. These students often benefit from special education programs. There, they get extra help in the areas where they're struggling. IQ tests can help teachers figure out which students would benefit from such extra help.

Chess is **a game of skill and strategy**. Intelligence helps, but so does really caring about it and having the perseverance to slowly **build skills** in it.

IQ tests also can help identify students who would do well in **fast-paced "gifted education" programs**. Many colleges and universities also use exams similar to IQ tests to select students. And the U. S. government — including its military — uses IQ tests when choosing who to hire. These tests help predict which people would make good leaders, or be better at certain specific skills.

It's tempting to read a lot into someone's IQ score. Most non-experts think intelligence is the reason successful people do so well. Psychologists who study intelligence find this is only partly true. IQ tests can predict how well people will do in particular situations, such as **thinking abstractly** in science, engineering or art, or leading teams of people. But there's more to the story. Extraordinary achievement depends on many things. And those extra categories include ambition, persistence, opportunity, the ability to think clearly — even luck.

Intelligence matters. But not as much as you might think.

IQ tests "measure a set of skills that are important to society," notes Scott Barry Kaufman. He's a psychologist at the University of Pennsylvania in Philadelphia. But, he adds, such tests don't tell the full story about someone's potential. One reason: IQ tests favor people who can **think on the spot.** It's a skill plenty of capable people lack.

Just being intelligent doesn't mean someone will be successful. And just because someone is less intelligent doesn't mean that person will fail. Most people believed intelligence and talent were important. But smart people don't always **live up to their potential.**

In the end, hard work can be just as important to success as IQ. "It's okay to struggle and go through setbacks," Kaufman says. It might not be easy. But over the long haul, **toughing it out** can lead to great accomplishments.

(Adapted from *sciencenewsforstudents.org*)

Opinion sharing

(a) Do you think you have a higher IQ or EQ? How can you tell?

(b) Do you think one can improve one's EQ? How?

(c) People with high IQ could both make great contributions and cause equal destruction. Do you agree? Why or why not?

(d) In addition to high IQ, what other qualities do you think a successful scientist should have? Why?

(e) On what occasions would you prefer to have a higher EQ?

Reference Words and Expressions

self-confidence	自信
non-aggressive	无侵犯性
self-worth and capabilities	自我价值和能力
recognize your own emotions	认清自己的情绪
manage disruptive impulses	管理破坏性冲动
maintain standards of honesty and integrity	保持诚实和正直的标准
handle change with flexibility	灵活处理变化
be open to new ideas	接受新思想
strive to meet a standard of excellence	努力达到卓越的标准
align with the goals of a group	与团队目标保持一致
ready yourself to act on opportunities	做好应对机遇的准备
pursue goals persistently despite obstacles	不顾障碍坚持不懈地追求目标
anticipate, recognize and meet clients' needs	预测、识别并满足客户的需求
sense what others need to progress	感觉到别人什么方面需要进步
cultivate opportunities through diverse people	通过不同的人来培养机会
read a group's emotional currents	了解一组人的情绪
power relationships	权力关系

discern the feelings behind the needs of others	洞察他人需求背后的感受
wield effective persuasion tactics	运用有效的说服策略
send clear messages	表达明确信息
inspire and guide groups	激励和引导团队
initiate or manage change	发起或处理变化
understand, negotiate and resolve	理解、协商和解决
build bonds	建立关系
conflict management	冲突管理
work with others towards shared goals	与他人一起努力实现共同的目标
create group synergy	创造团队协作
pursue collective goals	追求集体目标
exceptionally sensitive to touch, sound or light	对触摸、声音或光异常敏感
get lost in a book	沉浸在书本中
stay up late	熬夜
good instincts	良好的直觉
messy and disorganized	杂乱无章
enhance levels of creativity	提高创造力水平
intense focus on tasks	专注于任务
be easy to adapt to new environments	易于适应新的环境
prefer repetitive tasks	喜欢重复性任务
be flexible enough to go with the flow	灵活地顺应潮流
love learning	热爱学习
want to get ahead	想要出人头地
strong verbal communication skills	较强的口头沟通能力
be quick to notice changes	迅速注意到变化
a greater sense of intuition	更强烈的直觉
be naturally curious	天生好奇

Speaking Activities

Individual talk

Apart from EQ and IQ, there are a lot of quotients to gauge other aspects of human abilities such as adverse quotient, spiritual quotient and creative quotient. Talk about the application of these quotients in your life.

Share your opinions

When you are offered a highly-paid job and a further-education opportunity, which one would you choose? Why?

Situation analysis

IQ and EQ are both important factors contributing to the qualification of a job. Analyze the roles IQ and EQ play in the working process of each profession listed below.

teachers / managers / doctors / scientists

A3 Extensive Reading

How to Improve Your Emotional Intelligence: 7 Steps

Take an emotional intelligence test

First thing's first. Let's see where you stand on the spectrum of emotional intelligence. There are a lot of emotional intelligence tests online that you can take to help you understand your own EQ.

This test from the Global Leadership Foundation is a short, 40-question test that takes about 10 minutes. You only need to pick one out of two options given for each question that best describes you. For example:

"I always set myself challenging goals."

"I always complete the goals that are set for me."

Here is another test, provided by the Greater Good Science Center at the University of California, Berkeley. This option has only 25 questions, but each multiple choice has four answers to choose from.

Finally, this test from Psych Tests will take about an hour to complete and involves more reading and analyzing scenarios. It has a total of 341 questions, so while it will take more time and effort than the others, it may give you a more precise insight into your EQ.

Observe your feelings

So often in the chaos of the day, we lose touch with how we're feeling. To improve your EQ, you need to reconnect with your emotions and purposefully notice your mental state at various points of the day.

Set a timer to indicate when you need to take a minute to do this exercise so you aren't only doing it during your "down" times or rest periods. When you identify your emotion, look at your behavior as well. How are you acting when you experience this emotion, and how does that behavior impact your daily life? Being able to manage your emotions will become more natural once you recognize how you react to them. Also, the more you practice this trick of "catching" yourself throughout the day, the more you will become naturally mindful of your emotional state and its impact on your behavior.

Action Step: Set a timer on your phone or a reminder on your computer that will prompt you about 3-5 times throughout the day to stop what you're doing and be mindful of your current emotion. Acknowledge how that emotion is impacting your behavior at that time and accept full responsibility for both your feelings and your actions.

Question your opinions

Of course, this isn't something that people naturally do, because if you have an opinion or belief about something, it's likely you have accepted it as the truth. What's more, your opinions are often reinforced by the people around you who have similar viewpoints. But part of having a high EQ is having a willingness to see things from other people's perspectives. Don't become so set in your ways that you write off anyone else who may have a different opinion than you do about something.

Action Step: Be proactive in reading or looking into the "other side" of an issue. Allow your views to be challenged. Even if you still don't agree with another person's opinion on an issue, taking the time to hear an explanation will help you understand people who may think differently than you and ultimately make you more accepting of new ideas.

Find a way to pause

It's easy and immediately satisfying and rewarding in the moment to make a quick rude remark back to someone who said something that rubbed you the wrong way. But where does that ultimately get you? So often, we are reactive to stress or threats of harm, but these knee-jerk reactions never uncover a solution to the problem.

To control your emotions and avoid behavioral outbursts, take a minute to breathe. Walk outside to get some air, excuse yourself to get a drink of water, or simply tell the person you need to finish the discussion later. Figure out what works for you to help you maintain composure during stressful interactions so you can better absorb the situation and decide how to respond.

Let's look at an example. You just got a department-wide email about an issue at work and it seemed like the sender threw you under the bus. Your initial reaction may be to hit "reply all" with a strong defense (plus a diatribe) and hit "send" without even proofreading it.

But reacting in this careless manner would probably make the situation worse than it had to be and you could even do irreversible damage to your career, your professional relationships and your reputation at work.

However, if you give yourself some time to breathe and reflect, chances are you will think very differently about the situation and how you should handle it.

Action Step: When faced with a stressful situation, don't respond to anything in the heat of the moment. Figure out what your coping mechanism is for self-soothing and practice it. Only then should you formulate a response because your mind will be clear and your emotions will be calm.

Take an objective look at yourself

Because it's rather difficult to see yourself from an outsider's view, ask a few people who know you really well to tell you what they believe your strengths and weaknesses are. Don't argue if you disagree with what they say, just look for patterns in people's answers.

If you keep hearing from people that you have a habit of interrupting others while they're speaking or turning any conversation back to yourself, take that to heart. Being able to effectively listen to other people is a big part of having emotional intelligence, so this sort of feedback would suggest you have a big area for potential improvement.

Action Step: A good way to get an objective look at yourself is to keep a journal. At the end of each day, write down anything significant that happened, how it made you feel, and what actions you took in response. Documenting these details will help increase your awareness of your behaviors and potentially highlight where any issues could be coming from. Read back through your journal every once in a while, and highlight any trends you see.

Know your emotional triggers

Part of having self-awareness is being able to recognize your emotions and adapt them to any given situation. Most people have some sort of trigger — or "hot button"— that can initiate feelings of intense anger, hostility or irritation.

Almost anything could be a potential trigger for someone depending upon their values, beliefs and life experiences — from a particular viewpoint to simply a tone of voice. Being able to identify your emotional triggers is critical because without knowing what evokes an extreme response from you, you can easily let your emotions get the best of you.

Action Step: Whenever possible, if you feel as if you could face one of your triggers in an upcoming situation, think through the interaction and predict how you'll feel. Specify those feelings as best as you can and practice accepting them, which will help you regain control. Decide on an appropriate reaction to the feeling you identified and follow through with that plan if the situation arises.

Remember that it's a process

Don't forget that developing emotional intelligence is a process that you have to work on for your entire life. EQ is something you develop, and it requires continuous improvement. This is not something you can learn in a week or a month.

Action Step: As you're taking the steps listed above to improve your emotional intelligence, take note of your progress. It may seem like you don't see any tangible changes in your life right away, but with your daily practice, you will be able to see a big difference between your former self and your future self.

(Adapted from *developgoodhabits.com*)

Part B Gender and Age

B1. Introduction

Gender and Age

Definitions

AGE refers to the different stages in one's life cycle. It is important for protection programming to be aware of where people are in their life cycle as their capacities and needs change over time. Age influences, and can enhance or diminish, a person's capacity to exercise his or her rights. The protection risks affect an individual differently depending on age.

GENDER refers to the socially constructed roles for women, girls, men and boys. Gender roles are learned, changeable over time, and variable within and between cultures. Gender often defines the duties, responsibilities, constraints, opportunities and privileges of women, girls, men and boys in any context. Gender equality refers to the equal enjoyment of their rights, responsibilities and opportunities and it implies that the interests, needs and priorities of each gender are respected.

Gender roles and culture

Hofstede's research revealed that on the Masculinity and Femininity dimension, cultures with high masculinity reported distinct gender roles, moralistic views of sexuality and encouraged passive roles for women. Additionally, these cultures discourage premarital sex for women but have no such restrictions for men. The cultures with the highest masculinity scores were Japan, Italy, Austria and Venezuela. Cultures low in masculinity (high femininity) had gender roles that were more likely to overlap and encouraged more active roles for women. Sex before marriage was seen as acceptable for both women and men in these cultures. Four countries scoring lowest in masculinity were Norway, Denmark, Netherlands and Sweden. The United States is slightly more masculine than feminine on this dimension; however, these aspects of high masculinity are balanced by a need for individuality.

Stages of the human life

Which stage of life is the most important? Some might claim that infancy is the key stage, when a baby's brain is wide open to new experiences that will influence all the rest of its later life. Others might argue that it's adolescence or young adulthood, when physical health is at its peak. Many cultures around the world value late adulthood more than any other, arguing that it is at this stage that the human being has finally acquired the wisdom necessary to guide others. Who is right? The truth of the matter is that every stage of life is equally significant and necessary for the welfare of humanity. Each stage of life has its own unique "gift" to contribute to the world. We need to value each one of these gifts if we are to truly support the deepest needs of human life.

(Adapted from *globalprotectioncluster.org*; *maricopa.edu*; *institute4learning.com*)

B2. Passage Reading

B2.1 Gender

The following two passages focus on gender differences. Read and give your opinions according to the questions. Try to seek diverse perspectives and don't confine yourself to the reference words and expressions given.

Passage One

Society's Perspective of Men's Roles in the 21st Century

Thaddeus Howze

The roles of men haven't changed. Men are still expected to **bring home the bacon**, protect their families, be in charge of their family destiny and participate in society in a **dominant role**, guiding their offspring to the most successful outcomes possible.

However, society as a whole has changed while the perspective of men's roles has not. Society has deemed it improper to kill other social groups, members of other religion, to prevent other groups from having opportunities which could benefit them.

Advances of technology since the Industrial Age have all but destroyed the nature of men as **the primary provider**. Mechanization meant women were completely capable of participating in society more equally because when education was equal and training was equal, the outcomes of the Industrial Age also became equal.

The differences men enjoyed under the Agricultural Age where men's **physical strength** was a significant advantage, especially where **warfare** was concerned, as well as the socialized idea of protecting women from danger because they are the **progenitors** of the species, meant women were unable to participate in much of what society had to offer because men used their stature to **oppress women** (for a good reason, or so the excuse goes).

The very nature of gendered roles in an Information Age society has been rendered meaningless. With few exceptions, the truth of our civilization, whether sub-societies are willing to accept, is women are equal in every significant way to men. They have all the capacities men have enjoyed for centuries and they are unwilling to return to sitting at home and giving birth to children.

But **the converse** is also true. Men, who have, due to the opportunities they gave themselves, enjoyed dominance over the economic, cultural, social and traditional powers of society, have to accept this **hegemony** is coming to an end. Women are entering these circles of power and some room will have to be made. Men will have to broaden their horizons into what have been considered traditionally "women's work"— teaching, nursing, dental assisting, occupations where nurturing is a primary component — with the surprising discovery that they may find they can enjoy the work, enjoy the interaction, find themselves fulfilled in ways they may have never had the opportunity to experience in any other **social paradigm**. Men can be fully integrated into **the nurturing aspect** of our human capacity.

Change is our only universal constant. Our ability to adapt to change is what will save us from our social inertia, our reliance on tradition and culture, which were useful when we were developing and our technology changed at a generational pace, and culture and tradition were a means of adjusting slowly to a changing world. The pace of change, the **onslaught** of new technology means we have to adapt to new ways of thinking, new ways of seeing each other, new ways of accepting the new and different.

(Adapted from *goodmenproject. com*)

Passage Two

Why Are So Few Women in Leadership Roles?

Jillian Kramer

It's an unpleasant fact, but women are much less likely to **hold leadership positions** than men, and they're still having trouble **gaining ground**. "Despite gains in every profession, women remain underrepresented at all levels of leadership," according to a new report from the American Association of University Women. "In Congress, on corporate boards and in our nation's colleges and universities, male leaders **outnumber** female leaders by considerable margins."

Why, then, with so many talented and qualified women ready and willing to fill leadership roles, does a gender leadership gap even exist? The AAUW report offers a few explanations.

There's a pipeline problem.

Whether it's at the entry level or on the way to the C-Suite, **systemic barriers** exist that keep women stuck in place or out of a career field entirely. We know pipeline problems are the real deal thanks to a separate study that showed women are unable to enter, stuck in the middle, or locked out of the top of the technology sector to healthcare, retail, and several other career fields.

Sex discrimination is still happening.

According to the AAUW, "Some bias against women is **subtle**, but **overt** — and illegal — discrimination against women in the workplace remains an issue." The report shows that many companies still state a gender preference for select positions — in the 21st century! "This kind of illegal discrimination is not rare," the report states, with 30,000 cases of sex discrimination in the last five years alone resolving in favor of the person who filed the charge.

But women face sex discrimination outside of **the corporate world**, too. "In the political realm, rigid stereotypes about women and political leadership — often captured in **biased media coverage** of female candidates — can influence voters' perceptions of women candidates and discourage women from entering politics," the report states. Let's not forget how often questions about everything from Hillary Clinton's sexual orientation to her hairstyle choices have repeatedly surfaced.

And then, there's that whole work-life balance thing.

"Balancing work and family responsibilities is one of the most **challenging obstacles** for women seeking leadership positions," the AAUW report states. As the most-likely primary — or only — caregivers for their children, women often leave the workforce during their **peak employment years**. "They are more likely than men to work irregularly and spend time out of the workforce, and they are more likely to work part time," the report states.

What's more, women who would continue their careers after giving birth are often forced to quit their jobs because they aren't given **paid parental leave**. "When faced with the prospect of unpaid leave or no leave at all, many women who have children choose to leave the workforce," according to the AAUW. "Even when employers offer family-friendly policies, workers are reluctant to use them out of a concern that their work commitment will be questioned."

What can be done to level the leadership playing field for women? The problem won't require magic to fix, the AAUW assures us, but it will take a multi-step approach — one that includes everything from **diversity training** to employment practice reforms on college campuses, in corporations, and even in Congress.

Women themselves have a responsibility to **climb any leadership ladder** too. A separate study suggested that women must select their roles carefully — choosing positions that will lead to the C-Suite — and expand their career networks beyond other women to successful men. The pressure may still be on women to change a system set up against them, but we all know where the problems are — now we just have to fix them.

(Adapted from *glamour.com*)

☞ **Note**

The pipeline problem: It is a way for predominantly male leaders to talk about diversity in a way that avoids talking about this messy reality, not to mention the privileges they themselves have benefitted from. It's no accident that a pipeline is an engineering term, as engineers tend to run tech companies.

Opinion sharing

(a) From the above two passages, can you summarize the roles of man and woman in the society?
(b) What are the roles of your father and your mother in the family?
(c) In China, men highly outnumber women. Talk about the causes and consequences of this gender imbalance?
(d) From kindergarten to college, have you had more female teachers than male teachers? What do you think of this phenomenon?
(e) From your own perspective, what advantages does your gender have over the other?

Reference Words and Expressions

sexism	性别偏见(尤指对女性)
traditional male and female roles	传统男女角色
gender equality	两性平等
gender restrictions	性别限制
gender stereotypes	性别刻板印象
changing standards in society	不断变化的社会标准
dominant and protective	主导与保护
providers and protectors	提供者与保护者
provide for a family	养家糊口
source of financial security	财政保障来源
be strong, aggressive and bold	坚强、进取、大胆
being masculine	阳刚之气
create a cozy home	打造温馨的家
run the household	料理家务
nurture the children	养育孩子
source of emotional security	情感安全感的来源
self-sacrificing behaviors	自我牺牲的行为
typical feminine ways	典型的女性方式
be polite, accommodating and nurturing	礼貌、随和、有教养
take on responsibility	承担责任

equal ambitions	志向相同
equally capable	能力相当
regardless of gender	不分性别
expand one's role	扩大角色范围
glass ceilings	(女性职务升迁上遇到的)无形障碍
open up equal opportunities	开放平等机会
pursue a successful career	追求成功的事业
recognize the obstacles	认清障碍
gender pay gap	不同性别工资差异
opt out of further advancement	选择退出进一步的发展
hostile work conditions	不利的工作条件
take the lead	带头
create a new kind of teamwork	创造一种新的团队合作
traditionally considered to be men's domains	传统上被认为是男人的领域
eliminate the set gender roles	消除既定的性别角色

Speaking Activities

Read and discuss

Bride Price in China

Bride price has a long history in China. It has been one of the most important marriage customs in ancient China. In one small village north of Beijing, the average price that parents of sons would have to pay the parents of the potential bride was $38,000 — but the average yearly salary in the village was one-fifth that amount.

(Adapted from *bustle. com*)

Share your opinions:

(a) Is it fair for men to pay bride price before getting married?

(b) What do you think is the root for this custom?

(c) Is it reasonable to cancel the bride price?

Debate

Many people say that men are more stressed in a family because they are burdened with the pressure of making money and supporting the family. But others argue that women are more stressed because they usually have to work as well as take care of the family. What's your opinion?

Topic for debate: Who is more stressed in a family in China, husband or wife?

Read and discuss

Chinese Leftover Women

In Chinese culture, one of the goals in life is marriage and children. Once you're married, your life is successful. On the contrary, if you don't have a child and remain single, you'll be viewed as a "loser" in life. Leftover women may have started as a meaning of just someone unmarried over the age of 27, but has gone on to mean and express much more than that.

"Before, people thought women should marry early, otherwise they are left over," said a college student in Shanghai. "But now, it's OK if women put their career in first place, marriage in second or third place." Women are more free, able to live independently. This phenomenon is largely seen among the growing educated middle class.

(Adapted from *tutormandarin. net*)

Share your opinions on the following questions:

(a) Why are leftover women more commonly seen in China nowadays than before?

(b) What about leftover men? Do you think the reason for them to be single is the same as leftover ladies? Why or why not?

B2. 2 Age

The following two passages focus on age. Read and give your opinions according to the questions. Try to seek diverse perspectives and don't confine yourself to the reference words and expressions given.

Passage One

Old-age Is the Next Global Economic Threat

Noah Smith

While the world **wrestles with** a deadly pandemic and how to confront climate change, there's another, long-term global challenge that no one really knows how to deal with: **population aging**. As the human race transitions from a **burgeoning, exploding species** to a **static or shrinking** one, economies around the world will come under significant strain.

Japan is the canary in the coal mine here. Although its birth rate is not as low as that of many other rich countries, it's been low for a longer time. That's why Japan is now the world's oldest major economy.

On one hand, Japan demonstrates why a shrinking population doesn't automatically

impoverish a country. Its population is slowly declining, and is back down to the level of two decades ago, yet the country's income per capita has continued to rise as productivity grows and more women enter the workforce.

But **pronounced aging** like Japan's does come at an economic cost. Every year, a **dwindling pool** of working-age Japanese people is forced to support an **expanding pool** of grey-haired consumers. This is why Japan's living standards are falling behind rich countries with growing populations.

There's also another potential cost to severe aging: **macroeconomic dysfunction**. According to standard macroeconomic theory, every country has a natural rate of interest; when interest rates linger above this natural level, a country slips into a deflation. As Japan's population has **levelled off**, its economy has slipped into a seemingly permanent state of deflation or near-deflation.

Aging might also have another **subtle corrosive effect** on productivity. Especially in countries like Japan that promote people by seniority, a deficit of dynamic, fresh-thinking young people might make companies less nimble and less open to new ideas. Population shrinkage also saps the power of **economic agglomeration**, by making it harder to sustain a network of growing, productive cities.

Countries can, and do, try to compensate for population aging. Old people work longer, and more parents go to work instead of staying home with the kids. Countries also invest in automation; it's no accident that Japan has pushed hard to be a leader in the field of robotics. But unless robots get much better, there's probably a limit to how much these measures can **fight the greying tide**.

Societies like Japan are on the front lines of what will eventually be a global challenge. The human species has never before dealt with prolonged and continuous aging. Countries need to continue to aggressively search for solutions — especially technological fixes like automation — in order to ease this unprecedented transition.

(Adapted from *financialpost. com*)

Passage Two

Why Seniors Matter

Verena Menec

Stories abound in the media about how seniors are going to bankrupt the health care system or how the pension system will collapse **under the burden of** a growing senior population.

What we don't hear in the midst of all of these **doomsday stories** — which are not based in evidence, and are simply wrong — is how seniors contribute to society.

The fact that people live longer than ever should be celebrated as one of the biggest success stories in history. As the saying goes, "Getting old is better than the alternative."

How do seniors **contribute to society**? Like any younger person, they shop, they use services (which employ people), and they pay taxes. They also volunteer; in fact, many organizations would **be hard pressed to** function without their older volunteers.

Seniors also **give generously**: they make more **charitable donations** per capita than any other age group.

Seniors babysit; they look after grandchildren. One can only imagine what would happen to our economy if, suddenly, no grandparents were available to look after grandchildren. How many parents would have to **scramble to** find other care options (already scarce) — or would have to miss work because they couldn't find alternatives? How many soccer games or ballet classes would be missed if grandmas or grandpas were not there to drive the grandchildren?

Seniors do housework, home maintenance and yard work — not just for themselves, but for others as well. They provide transportation or **run errands** for others. They provide emotional support and friendship, like the senior who looks in on a house-bound friend to make sure that everything is alright and stays for a chat.

Seniors provide care for spouses or friends. Think of the wife who **takes on** more and more responsibilities in and outside the home as her husband starts to get frail. She may not think of herself as a caregiver, but without her, what would happen to him? Who would get the groceries, run errands, do the cooking, take him to medical appointments?

Other family members are not always available to help. They may live too far away or have health problems themselves. There are organizations that can help out — but the bulk of these supports are made possible because of volunteers.

And the volunteers are typically seniors.

Then there is the husband who takes care of his wife who has Alzheimer's, who, from moment to moment, can no longer remember what day of the week it is, never mind what month or year, whether she has eaten, or what she just did; who keeps asking the same question over and over again, forgetting the answer as soon as it is given. He makes sure she gets dressed, eats properly, takes her medication, accompanies her to the doctor, and keeps her life as normal as possible. Without him, she would not be able to live at home anymore, but would have to **be admitted to a care home.**

Because of him, she is able to stay in familiar surroundings for as long as possible. Because of him, she is not a "burden" on the health care system.

Rather than creating **catastrophic visions** of the impact of the "**gray tsunami**", it would help if we took a more balanced approach to the aging population. We need policy solutions to address the real challenges, such as: How do we ensure that family and friends who care for older adults and play such an important role in their lives receive the supports they need? How do we provide supports in communities to make them as **age-friendly** as possible so that seniors can continue to contribute to society and have the best quality of life?

Acknowledging seniors' contributions would help to make ours a more **age-inclusive society** that does not pit one generation against the other. It would also be a more accurate reflection of how most of us engage with each other in our everyday lives.

(Adapted from *evidencenetwork. ca*)

Opinion sharing

(a) What problems might occur in an aging society? Summarize the points in passage one.
(b) What part do typical Chinese grandparents play in a family? What would happen if they were not around?
(c) Many retired people are highly educated professionals. How can our government make use of these human resources?
(d) When you get older, would you rather live in a nursing home or stay with your children? Why?
(e) What do you think of the two-child policy in China? Is it a solution to the aging problem?

Reference Words and Expressions

Silent and Older	老去的沉默世代(1946 年以前出生)
baby boomers	婴儿潮一代(1946～1964 年出生)
Gen X	X 世代(1965～1980 年出生)
Millennial	千禧年世代(1981～1996 年出生)
Gen Z	Z 世代(1996 年以后出生)
over the course of life	在一生中
life cycle	生命周期
life span	寿命
life expectancy	预期寿命
mimic what you see others do	模仿别人的行为
be dependent on parents	依赖父母

grow rapidly	迅速成长
pick up life skills	学习生活技能
deal with more difficult tasks	处理更困难的任务
immature juvenile	幼年
mature into adults	长大成人
senior citizen	老年人
health issues	健康问题
concerns about aging	对老龄化的担忧
provide guidance	提供指导
decision-making	做决定
blueprint of life	人生蓝图
be accepted by society	被社会接受
mold the way we think	塑造我们的思维方式
late adolescence	青春期晚期
early adulthood	成年早期
coming of age	成年
absorb knowledge from others	从别人那里学习知识
copy actions	模仿他人行为
fit in	融入
discover who we really are	认识真正的自我
learn from trial and error	从试错中学习
experiment with all sorts of activities	尝试各种活动
manage relationships	管理各种关系
party with friends	和朋友聚会
recognize your limitations	认识到你的不足
evaluate what you are good at	评估己之所长
cut away unimportant aspects of life	去掉生活中不重要的部分
get serious about the things you have	认真对待你所拥有的东西
accomplish all you can	尽你所能
remain driven and determined	保持动力和决心
invest in oneself	自我投资
experience a turbulent life	经历动荡的生活
filled with adventure and misfortune	充满了冒险和不幸
culmination of a life	生命的顶点
pass down legacy to the next generation	把遗产传给下一代
find meaning in life and death	发现生死的意义
age is not just a number, it's a privilege	年龄不仅是个数字，更是一种特权
reshape demographics	重塑人口结构

set off alarm bells	敲响警钟
normal retirement age	正常退休年龄
population pyramid	人口金字塔
low fertility rate	低生育率
age distribution	年龄分布

Speaking Activities

Discussion

As we all know, the major stages of life are childhood, adolescence, adulthood and old age. How would you put them in the order of importance? Why?

Read and debate

According to statistics in the U. S. in 2015, juveniles (<18 years old) accounted for 10.2% of all violent crime arrests and 14.3% of all property crime arrests. 605 juveniles (<18 years old) were arrested for murder, 2,745 for forcible rape, and 21,993 for aggravated assault.

(Adapted from *cdc. gov*)

Topic for debate: Should juveniles who commit violent crimes be treated as adults?

Debate

Should Gifted Children Be Separated?

There is a hot debate over the separation of the gifted children — the ones who are extremely bright, talented or special from those who aren't. Some people advocate for the separation while others don't.

(Adapted from *imafulltimemummy. com*)

Topic for debate: Gifted children should be educated separately from non-gifted children.

B3. Extensive Reading

The Twelve Stages of the Human Life Cycle

Thomas Armstrong

Which stage of life is the most important? The truth of the matter is that every stage of life is equally significant and necessary for the welfare of humanity.

Prebirth

Potential — The child who has not yet been born could become anything — a Michelangelo, a Shakespeare, a Martin Luther King — and thus holds for all of humanity the principle of what we all may yet become in our lives.

Birth

Hope — When a child is born, it instills in its parents and other caregivers a sense of optimism; a sense that this new life may bring something new and special into the world. Hence, the newborn represents the sense of hope that we all nourish inside of ourselves to make the world a better place.

Infancy (Ages 0-3)

Vitality — The infant is a vibrant and seemingly unlimited source of energy. Babies thus represent the inner dynamo of humanity, ever fueling the fires of the human life cycle with new channels of psychic power.

Early Childhood (Ages 4-6)

Playfulness — When young children play, they recreate the world anew. They take what is and combine it with what is possible to fashion events that have never been seen before in the history of the world. As such, they embody the principle of innovation and transformation that underlies every single creative act that has occurred in the course of civilization.

Middle Childhood (Ages 7-8)

Imagination — In middle childhood, the sense of an inner subjective self develops for the first time, and this self is alive with images taken in from the outer world, and brought up from the depths of the unconscious. This imagination serves as a source of creative inspiration in later life for artists, writers, scientists, and anyone else who finds their days and nights enriched for having nurtured a deep inner life.

Late Childhood (Ages 9-11)

Ingenuity — Older children have acquired a wide range of social and technical skills that enable them to come up with marvelous strategies and inventive solutions for dealing with the increasing pressures that society places on them. This principle of ingenuity lives on in that part of ourselves that ever seeks new ways to solve practical problems and copes with everyday responsibilities.

Adolescence (Ages 12-20)

Passion — The biological event of puberty unleashes a powerful set of changes in the adolescent body that reflect themselves in a teenager's sexual, emotional, cultural and / or spiritual passion. Adolescence passion thus represents a significant touchstone for anyone who is seeking to reconnect with their deepest inner zeal for life.

Early Adulthood (Ages 21-35)

Enterprise — It takes enterprise for young adults to accomplish their many responsibilities, including finding a home and mate, establishing a family or circle of friends, and / or getting a good job. This principle of enterprise thus serves us at any stage of life when we need to go out into the world and make our mark.

Midlife (Ages 36-50)

Contemplation — After many years in young adulthood of following society's scripts for creating a life, people in midlife often take a break from worldly responsibilities to reflect upon the deeper meaning of their lives. This element of contemplation represents an important resource that we can all draw upon to deepen and enrich our lives at any age.

Mature Adulthood (Ages 51-80)

Benevolence — Those in mature adulthood have raised families, established themselves in their work life, and become contributors to the betterment of society through volunteerism, mentorships and other forms of philanthropy. All of humanity benefits from their benevolence. Moreover, we all can learn from their example to give more of ourselves to others.

Late Adulthood (Age 80+)

Wisdom — Those with long lives have acquired a rich repository of experiences that they can use to help guide others. Elders thus represent the source of wisdom that exists in each of us, helping us to avoid the mistakes of the past while reaping the benefits of life's lessons.

Death & Dying

Life — Those in our lives who are dying, or who have died, teach us about the value of living. They remind us not to take our lives for granted, but to live each moment of life to its fullest, and to remember that our own small lives form a greater whole.

Since each stage of life has its own unique gift to give to humanity, we need to do whatever we can to support each stage, and to protect each stage from attempts to suppress its individual contribution to the human life cycle. Thus, we need to be wary, for example, of attempts to thwart a young child's need to play through the establishment high-pressure formal academic preschools. We should protect the wisdom of aged from elder abuse. We need to do what we can to help our adolescents at risk. We need to advocate for prenatal education and services for poor mothers, and support safe and healthy birthing methods in third world countries. We ought to take the same attitude toward nurturing the human life cycle as we do toward saving the environment from global warming and industrial pollutants. For by supporting each stage of the human life cycle, we will help to ensure that all its members are given care and helped to blossom to their fullest degree.

(Adapted from *institute 4learning. com*)

References

Personality Types. *They Differ*. Retrieved from https://theydiffer. com/difference-between-introvert-and-extrovert-personality-types/ on March 15th, 2021.

What Is Emotional Intelligence (EQ)? *Psych Central*. Retrieved from https://psychcentral. com/lib/what-is-emotional-intelligence-eq#3 on March 15th, 2021.

Dr. Edwin van Thiel. (2019). Intelligence Quotient. 123 *Test*. Retrieved from https://www. 123test. com/what-is-iq-what-is-intelligence/ on March 15th, 2021.

Sally Percy. (2019). Do Extroverts Make Better Leaders? *Forbes*. Retrieved from https://www. forbes. com/sites/sallypercy/2019/06/10/do-extroverts-make-better-leaders/? sh=70effaa56fe2 on March 15th, 2021.

Kathy Caprino. (2017). Bias Against Introverts. *Forbes*. Retrieved from https://www. forbes. com/sites/kathycaprino/2017/12/29/im-sick-of-our-cultures-bias-against-introverts-and-im-ashamed-to-admit-i-have-one/#11c92e24d50d on March 15th, 2021.

S. Surbhi (2017). Personality vs. Character. *Key Differences*. Retrieved from https://keydifferences. com/difference-between-personality-and-character. html on March 15th, 2021.

Stephanie Burns. (2020). Engage Emotional Intelligence to Better Your Relationships. *Forbes*. Retrieved from https://www. forbes. com/sites/stephanieburns/2020/04/11/engage-emotional-intelligence-to-better-your-relationships-and-expand-your-influence/ on March 15th, 2021.

Alison Pearce Stevens. (2016). How Much Does IQ Matter? *Science News for Students*. Retrieved from https://www. sciencenewsforstudents. org/article/what-iq-and-how-much-does-it-matter on March 15th, 2021.

How to Improve Your Emotional Intelligence: 7 Steps. *Develop Good Habits*. Retrieved from https://www. developgoodhabits. com/emotional-intelligence/ on March 15th, 2021.

Gender and Age. *Global Protection Cluster*. Retrieved from https://www. globalprotection-cluster. org/themes/age-gender-diversity/ on March 15th, 2021.

Gender Roles and Culture. *Maricopa*. Retrieved from https://open. maricopa. edu/culturepsychology/chapter/gender-roles-and-culture/ on March 15th, 2021.

Thomas Armstrong. The Twelve Stages of the Human Life Cycle. *Institute 4 Learning*. Retrieved from https://www. institute4learning. com/resources/articles/the-12-stages-of-life/ on March 15th, 2021.

Thaddeus Howze. (2018). Society's Perspective of Men's Roles in the 21st Century.

The Good Man Project. Retrieved from https://goodmenproject.com/featured-content/societys-perspective-mens-roles-21st-century-lbkr/ on March 15th, 2021.

Jillian Kramer. (2016). Why Are So Few Women in Leadership Roles? *Glamour*. Retrieved from https://www.glamour.com/story/why-are-so-few-women-in-leader on March 15th, 2021.

Lani Seelinger. (2018). "Bride Price" in China. *Bustle*. Retrieved from https://www.bustle.com/p/theres-still-a-bride-price-in-china-its-actually-going-up-12012639 on March 15th, 2021.

Chinese Leftover Women. (2017). *Tutor Mandarin*. Retrieved from https://www.tutormandarin.net/en/leftover-women/, on March 15th, 2021.

Noah Smith. (2020). Old-age Is the Next Global Economic Threat. *Financial Post*. Retrieved from https://financialpost.com/news/economy/old-age-is-the-next-global-economic-threat on March 15th, 2021.

Verena Menec. (2012). Why Seniors Matter. *Evidence Network*. Retrieved from http://evidencenetwork.ca/why-seniors-matter-and-how-they-contribute-to-our-everyday-lives-2/.

Youth Violence. *CDC*. Retrieved from https://www.cdc.gov/violenceprevention/pdf/yv-datasheet.pdf on March 15th, 2021.

Should Gifted Children Be Separated? (2012). *I'm a Full-Time Mummy*. Retrieved from http://www.imafulltimemummy.com/post/2012/09/22/Should-Gifted-Children-Be-Separated.aspx on March 15th, 2021.

Thomas Armstrong. The Twelve Stages of the Human Life Cycle. *Institute For Learning*. Retrieved from https://www.institute4learning.com/resources/articles/the-12-stages-of-life/ on March 15th, 2021.